ANNA LE PLEY TAYLOR

Heartbreakingly Beautiful

A Story of Surrender, Hope, and Four Children Who Became A Family

To my four blessings and the women who gave them to me.

Contents

Acknowledgments

Do you know how hard it is to write anything, let alone a book, while young children are present? So this pouring out of my heart would not have been possible if it weren't for Jon. He carried more than his fair share many, many Saturdays and evenings so I could pour my heart onto these pages. He spent countless date nights listening to me work through my thoughts, trying to bring clarity to what I'd wanted to say. He made coffee, dinners, and cocktails, while I ignored everything attempting to put into words what was living in my mind. And most importantly, he supported my desires to share the intimate details of our process and our lives, allowing us to be completely vulnerable with you.

Long before there was a supportive husband and darling children, there was my mother. She has been my biggest fan and advocate for my dreams. Her steadying words of wisdom have guided me through some of the harder parts of this story. Often people go looking for mentors, but I have one in my mother. Thank you, Mama, for helping me see God's grace when my vision was clouded and for always believing He had a bigger story for me.

And, of course, this book would not exist if it wasn't for the selfless birth mothers who chose us and bravely placed their babies in our arms. Babies we will love fiercely and deeply until the day we die. Thank you, I will never be able to fully put into words the magnitude of the blessings you've given us.

For it is all for your sake, so that as grace extends to more and more people it may increase thanksgiving, to the glory of God. ~ 2 Corinthians 4:15

Introduction

I sat at the kitchen table, tears streaming down my 17-year-old face, devastated at what was laid out before me. The late afternoon April light not doing anything to warm my heartbroken soul. Nine, *nine*, rejection letters, all received and opened on the same day, were spread out on the table. Not one envelope had contained that fat, heavy feel of acceptance. All of them had been thin and dismissive form letters sent to those who did not make the cut. I had not made the cut, even though I had been promised otherwise. I had worked hard, planned and expected I would be accepted by at least *one* of them. It felt as though the rug had been pulled out from under me. I felt place-less. Lost. Without vision or hope for what lay ahead. My future dreams fell right alongside my tears.

But, God's will is *never* what you expect.

Well, that's awesome. How discouraging and depressing. How utterly opposite of what I wanted to hear to lift my spirits and carry me forward. But wait, hear me out. God's will is *never* what we expect *and* this is a good thing. Why would we want to limit our expectations to our finite, limited, inexperienced ideas rather than God's vast creative and knowledgeable vision?

For example, what if *my* grand plans were to go to a certain type of small liberal arts college on the East Coast and apply to nine schools

1

with guarantees from many that I would be accepted? Then what if, on that one fateful day in April I received not one, not two, but all *nine* rejection letters back from these same colleges? And what if, at this point, it was way late in the season to apply for a good college and receive a financial package that I desperately needed in order to be able to attend this type of school? And what if an acquaintance suggested I try a college I hadn't even considered before, but checked all the boxes of what I was looking for? And what if I called them, asked if I could apply and boldly asked after financial assistance? And what if I was both accepted almost immediately and also given a generous financial package that allowed me to attend this particular liberal arts college on the East Coast? And what if this particularly stressful month in April of my senior year of high school set me on a path that would result 20 years later in the adoption of four beautiful children?

Wait. Hold up. How did we get from college applications to adoption? That's the entire point of this story. The trajectory of my life was changed because of what God had planned. The experiences I had in that twenty-year journey were far beyond the expectations I had set out for myself. Above and beyond what I had expected, God had planned. If God done what *I* expected, I would have attended one of the nine schools I had applied to - but then I wouldn't have met the strategic relationships that set me down the next steps of God's plan. My plan would have set me down a path that would have *missed* the biggest blessings of my life. This God-designed journey began 20 years before I saw the most beautiful part of my story unfold. But if I hadn't been so severely rejected, I can confidently say I wouldn't have four beautiful adopted children. Some call this fate, destiny, astral influence. I call it God.

Hollywood loves this type of thing. These are the stories that movies are made from - twists and turns of fate that lead the character down surprisingly and gloriously unexpected pathways.That is exactly what I'm getting at. We all crave unanticipated movie-like experiences. It is the reason we are so attracted to great films in the first place. They are bigger than our imaginations, wilder than our dreams, and we wish it would happen to us. That is what God's will looks like. It is bigger than our imagination, more untamed, even feral, a little bit dangerous, sometimes heartbreaking, life-giving, and always unexpected.

That is what makes it amazing.

That is also what makes it incredibly frustrating, irritatingly depressing, anger-inducing, and downright maddening. Why, if God's will is supposed to be amazing, do we often have this adverse response to it? Let me give you a little hint, it's a control thing. Unfortunately for us, we crave control. We like to know what is going to happen, when it is going to take place, who is going to be there, and what is in it for us. We like to know what to expect, how we can plan, and all the other various factors that give us the illusion that we can control our little part of the world. And that is just the thing that smacks against us when we face the will of God. We want to be able to expect something, plan for it, and even anticipate the highs and lows so we can prepare our hearts.

But that's exactly what I'm talking about. It is not the way it works. If a movie was predictable and you knew what was going to happen you would not be as interested in watching it. It's in the unpredictability, the unexpected, the unanticipated twists and turns, that actually draw you into the story and keep you on the edge of your seat. They are what cause your heart to be invested and tears to fall when you least expect them. They are what cause you to be angry and frustrated and yet elated and ecstatic - all within the same ninety minutes of the simple story that you didn't write and has no effect on your life.

Now imagine this is your life. But years and years of a story unfolding. God's will is not chaotic and nor confusing, but it is outside of our limited purview. It is being woven years before it unfolds. Before the most beautiful part of the story is revealed, the groundwork was set in place decades ago. This is what makes it fabulous. It means that what seemingly feels like chaos, unpredictability, heartbreak, disappointment, and frustration can, in fact, become beautiful pieces of our story. They can be the pieces that mold us and shape us into who we are. They can be the pieces that become the best parts of our story, we just can't see it yet.

So here is what I'm telling you about this book. This book is the story of how I had to learn, over and over again, to let go of control and my expectations so that the blessings and beautiful story that God was writing could become what I saw instead of the flat, colorless version I was trying to write for myself. I had to be rejected from nine colleges to be set on the path that led me to adopt four children. The story God has for each of us is spectacular and the sooner we realize that everything comes together for that story, the more beautiful our life is. My story led me to four beautiful adopted children. Where is yours leading?

1

The Moment My World Changed

The energy in the room is excitedly nervous, surprisingly peaceful, and yet expectant. Nurses move about with encouraging words and precise movements. There is a growing, palpable tension, and painful cries fill the space. Then a release and the room lets out a breath it didn't know it was holding. Tiny cries break through the air and a wet, messy, and tiny body is placed in my arms. Not the arms of the one who carried her in her womb, but my arms.

Then my world goes still.

There is plenty of movement around me, but I am lost to the little person in my arms. She stills, not crying anymore, nestled against my skin. Incredulous joy fills my heart. And an overwhelming sadness follows quickly on its heels. I am suddenly fully aware of the gentle woman across the room who is being attended to by the nurses. Being cleaned up, encouraged, and made comfortable. Her eyes catch mine, exhausted but clear. She offers me a smile which I return. And then our worlds start swirling in different directions. One incredibly intimate moment between two strangers. One breathtaking moment. One overwhelming selfless gift lies in my arms: a baby given to me by her mother.

The journey of adoption rips you apart, has you on your knees, lays you bare. We were changed profoundly by our experience. Not just once, not twice, but four times. *Four times*. We subjected ourselves to the most raw journey we've ever experienced four times. Why? Why would we do that to ourselves? Because the journey is one of surrender, awe, and blessing. It has also been the most intimate example of God's love we have ever experienced. In short, it is heartbreakingly beautiful.

Let's start back at the beginning.

2

The Produce Aisle

I stood next to the carrots and celery, with a bunch of cilantro in my hand, trying to remember the exact recipe when a friend of my mother's approached me to congratulate me on my recent marriage. This was a common experience, as the valley I grew up in was small, and one could never go to the grocery store without running into someone they knew. I smiled thanking her and then the predictable barrage of questions followed.

My husband and I married "later in life" as people so *gently* like to tell you. We had both experienced a world full of living before marrying, Jon at 30 and me at the ripe old age of 33. Marrying later, when seemingly everyone else was well on their way in life, came with the onslaught of questions about when we were going to start a family and usually followed by some unsolicited advice on the best way to accomplish said task. Usually their opinion was heavily laced with the idea 'we'd better get on it since I was so *old*' - 33 people, 33! Since when is 33 old?.

So there I was, trapped up against the organic carrots with a bunch of wet cilantro sticking to my fingers, listening to a lovely woman from my mother's Bible study, of all places, explain how standing on my head might do the trick - or elevating your hips for 20 minutes! If you have no idea what I'm talking about, I hope you don't come into understanding in a small local grocery store caught between the carrots and the celery. And I wish I could say this was a solitary instance, but that would be too easy. No, the cross we would bear by not marrying young and not starting a family the traditional way, would be more than our fair share of awkward and vulnerable conversations. But I digress, and actually, this is not even the true beginning.

To get to this uncomfortable grocery store experience, where sex advice was offered over the organic produce, both my husband and I took long, meandering journeys that led us to this point Looking back now, I realize all those years before we married were preparation for what was ahead (aren't they always?). We would learn that our willingness to be vulnerable and honest about our lives, trusting God's hand would always go before us, would open doors we didn't even know existed. God had been planting seeds of trusting him long before adoption even came into the picture. He had been building trust, obedience, faith and every other trait needed for us to release control and surrender our future family to his plans. But of course we were blind to all this faith-building while it transpired. I was repeatedly held captive by my own spiraling expectations of 'but this has happened to everyone but me' and other comparative narratives. After I attended my seventh wedding of the season solo, or a birth announcement would come in the mail and I would be stuck in that uncomfortable place between happy and jealous.

I came from a large loving family of four sisters, and an even larger extended family with dozens of loving aunts, uncles, and cousins. Big beautiful families were life to me; the most important thing in the world. I was raised to respect and love my parents and my siblings. My mother would insist on forced family fun, as we would call it, a purposeful time where we would spend hours together as a family. We were raised to believe your family was the most important set of people in your world. It was deeply ingrained in me to crave this family connection and desire to build one of my own.

Ever since I was a little girl, I dreamed of my own family and played house regularly. And I *loved* babies. I have an early memory from when I was about five years old, sitting on the floor of my room playing with baby dolls and praying to God that my boobs would work so I could feed my baby dolls. I wanted to nurse them like I had seen my mother feed my youngest sister. That same 5-year-old mind was also convinced that I wanted to run an orphanage, so I would line up all my dollies and stuffies and tuck them into each of their beds. My only references for an orphanage were movies and storybooks (cue Annie), but of course I was going to be nice like Grace and not mean like Mrs. Hannigan. Thanks to these fairy tales and movies, my 5-year-old visions for my life went as follows: get married to prince charming, have lots of babies, and of course live in a castle with talking animals. Realistic dreams for sure.

As I grew older, the specific details changed, but the underlying desires of my heart remained the same. But by middle school I desperately wanted to appear cool and stuffed those childhood dreams away. And by the time I hit the high school drama, I had forgotten all about my castle orphanage filled with babies. But here's the thing, now I see that a vision was being planted deep in my soul by God. A vision of a house full of children who needed to be unconditionally loved. A desire to live side by side in this chaos with a partner in crime. The vision of stairs filled with running feet, laughter as little bodies jumped from bed to bed, and the unhinged joy that comes from chaos in the safety of your fortress, your castle.

The madness of senior year, college applications, and future planning rekindled my childhood dreams. The desire to marry and start a family became the central motivator for selecting what type of college I wanted to attend. I visited schools eyes wide to what species of males I might catch. And, in my enthusiasm for my future dreams, I applied to nine small liberal arts colleges on the East Coast. Being from California, I was obsessed with anything *but* Californian males. I schemed and I planned, visiting each of these nine schools and being reassured by the admissions staff that I was a "shoo-in" with my good grades, extra-curricular activities, and of course my Californian vibes. I could already envision my future, studying amongst the ivy-clad brick buildings, weathering the winter snow, falling hopelessly in love with a sweater-wearing, lacrosse-playing, fraternity boy named Graham. I had it all planned.

And then, *and then*, it all fell apart. One fateful day in April of my senior year, after most of my friends had confirmed their college of choice, I received all nine rejection letters back from my chosen schools. *All nine*. In. One. Day. I was devastated, confused, crushed and suddenly unmoored. I couldn't see beyond what I had planned, what I had expected. After the tears dried and multiple cups of tea consumed, clarity began to settle in.

Over my high school years, my faith had built slowly and steadily. It was theoretical, not practical. My faith had never directly impacted my life in such a blatant manner. And here's what I mean, God had other plans for me. I had busily gone about planning my future and

10

had not paused long enough to consider what God might have planned for me. I had good ideas. I was going to go to a well-respected liberal arts college, to get a degree in business, to find a suitable spouse, and settle down and have kids. These were sound plans. But these plans had not included God and in order to get my attention he had to make a big statement. See, if He had let one or two of these colleges accept me, I would have run off and carried on with my plans. But no. To stop me in my tracks and redirect me, it had to be memorable. And so, when the tears had dried and the teapot emptied, I remembered that God had a bigger plan for me. One I couldn't yet see, but I needed to trust him. This would be the first in many, many times I would learn and relearn this lesson. The first of many times I would relinquish my dreams, let go of control and wait to see the bigger picture. Apparently I was a slow learner.

After high school I left our small, sheltered valley for a Christian college across the country and my childhood dreams returned. The environment of the Christian college, intended or not, encouraged early marriage and big families, so that's what I heartily embraced. I was convinced I'd be married by graduation and start in on my big family, just as I'd seen countless others before me do. I wanted to be that young 25-year-old mom with the gaggle of kids. The mom everyone thinks is the nanny because they're so young and hot. Every guy I met was a potential Prince Charming - whether or not they wanted to be was of no importance to me. I was convinced I would find my soulmate, my better half, my helpmate, my kindred spirit, my every-other-Hallmark Christmas movie title you can imagine. My 20-year-old self was attending college to find a husband, my degree was just a byproduct of my hunt.

I managed almost all four years of school without a single boyfriend.

Not one. Maybe they could sense the determination of the hunt from a mile away and gave me a wide berth, or perhaps the stench of my desperation was little intense, but I like to think (go with me on this and let me keep some dignity) that God was protecting me from myself. He knew I wasn't ready for what He had planned. Just as He knew I wouldn't have jumped at the opportunity to attend one of the many colleges I had selected, He also knew I would jump at the first opportunity to marry the first Prince Charming who asked, no matter how ill-suited we were for each other. The thing is, He knew me and my desires. He *knew* and He had already gone before me with a plan. He knew I needed refining for what lay ahead. Twenty years of refinement before I was ready to embrace wholeheartedly the gifts He would bestow upon me. Gifts beyond my wildest expectations. But first I had to weather disappointment, feelings of failure, and the letting go of my own dreams.

3

The Journey to Prince Charming

F our years without a boyfriend in college was *almost* true.
He was six feet tall with blonde hair and blue eyes. An
infectious smile and magnetic smile. He was outgoing,
spontaneous, dynamic and he was God-ordained for sure. He was
my perfect other half.

I finally managed to snare this unsuspecting man in the last few months
of my senior year (just in the nick of time to meet my self-imposed
arbitrary deadline), and now I could happily attend all my friends'
weddings with a boyfriend on my arm. And this wasn't just any
boyfriend. This boy *had been looking for me* for three years. You see,
back in the early years of school I was so incredibly homesick that
my sister convinced me to work at a Christian camp with her for the
summer, where I met said boy-let's just call him Matt for the sake of
this story (definitely *not* his name).

Matt had a girlfriend at the time so I never considered him as a
possibility as I perused the camp staff, considering my options for
marriageable men. But apparently I had left quite an impression on

him. And for the three years after we had worked together at the camp, he tried unsuccessfully to track me down. It wasn't until my senior year of college, when I needed to fulfill a science credit requirement and attended a winter Biology Study program in a remote corner of Michigan, that he found me. I arrived at the program in the dead of winter, in January, to be met by a lovely couple who quickly realized that *this* was the Anna from California their friend Matt had been looking for over the past three years. It felt like fate-like God's hand had finally placed in my lap "the one" I was to marry. I mean, how storybook could this possibly be? Boy searches for girl for three years only to have her turn up in the remote edges of Michigan. He sweeps her off her feet, teaches her how to kiss (oh, did I not mention I also had never been kissed?), and then moves her down to Atlanta with the intentions of marriage. He most definitely wasn't repelled by my dreams to marry and settle down, and actually, it seemed like this was God making His plans unmistakably clear to us as we were swept up in a whirlwind towards marriage. How could we possibly deny it? So, I picked up and moved to Atlanta to be near him and his job and so I could secure that diamond ring. We were a dynamic pair. He was charismatic, charming, and fun. I was fresh out of college, lively, not sure of myself and who I was becoming, and desperate to get married.

Wait. That doesn't sound right.

But no matter, he asked my dad for my hand and secured a family heirloom ring for me. But God had other plans (bet you saw that coming, didn't you?). And thankfully my brother-in-law pulled this lovely Prince Charming aside before he could propose and helped him to see how we were not well matched. You might be wondering why my brother-in-law didn't pull his own sister-in-law (aka me) aside to enlighten her? Well, she would not have any of the enlightening. She was blind to anything but her stubborn plan. I was so focused on my vision of being married young that I didn't see the warning signs of being poorly matched. Hear me when I say there was nothing wrong with dear old Matt. He was (and I assume, still is) a wonderful person. But he was not the wonderful person for me. I was a scribbled shape of a person, with sharp points and undefined edges. I needed refining. I would have made a terrible wife for anyone at that point in time as I would have sought my identity from my role as wife and mother and not from God. I had placed too much importance on a marriage and building a family (I'm sure you couldn't tell), to be healthy in a relationship. God wanted more for me. I needed shaping and molding before I could carry the vision that God had for me. *But,* he used that relationship to move me to Atlanta, which happened to be pivotal and necessary for the next phase of my life. It was a thread that I would not see woven into my cloth of life until much later, but it was significant for my growth.

As that important relationship fell apart, leaving me stranded in an unknown city with very few friends, so did my dreams of marrying young and starting a family. My roommates from college had already married and started in on those dreams. My oldest sister had already married and started down that same road and I started to feel left behind. Even the new friends I had made in my short time in Atlanta were marrying off. I started to feel like the only person on the dance floor when they asked for all the single ladies for the bouquet toss. Mind you, I wasn't the only person on that dance floor, but the crowd started to thin as the years went by and I *felt* like it was just me out there, still waiting. When I had moved from Boston to Atlanta, I had secured a job working at a large church-with a massive single's group, of all things. I mean 3,000 single people every week. But I had started that job convinced I would be married within the year, so those single people were not my people. *I* was different, *I* had a boyfriend, *I* didn't need the singles group.

And then suddenly I was them and it terrified me.

I was no longer a college student, I was no longer in a relationship. Now I was a "single" person and all the stigmas that came with that. This would be the first time I would be faced with one of my largest fears-remaining single forever and ever amen. I would learn that God's plan was outside of my limited perspective. I was heartbroken and devastated that my dream boy had broken up with me. I had a harder time letting go of our perfect story than letting go of the boy himself, as it had seemed so much like God's plan. It felt like God had moved me to Atlanta and then abandoned me there with a bunch of desperate, single people. (If you recall, I could probably give them a run for their money in the desperation category). My first inclination was to pick up and move back to Boston or home to California. But I had a little nudging deep in my soul that said I needed to stay. I needed to confront this fear I had of being, and potentially, remaining single. I was beginning to hear and *listen* to the still small voice of God, the same one that had been directing my steps all this time. I was just getting better at listening.

In the remaining year and a half that I spent working with this singles group, and being single, I learned something that would be stuck to me for the next ten years that would prove to be invaluable when were were later faced with infertility.

Empathy.

I learned empathy. It sounds so simple and obvious, but until that moment when I felt abandoned in a new city and so very single, I had not stopped to consider how many others felt just like I did-and probably had been feeling that way for a lot longer than I had. Suddenly I identified with this group of "singles"-a category that seemed to be pariah in our sheltered Christian society. *They hadn't managed to secure a significant other, something must be wrong with them.* Wrong with *me*. It was jarring to realize my own stereotype had clouded my perspective of an entire demographic in our country. A valuable, dynamic, and very, very misunderstood demographic. Empathy was hard lesson to learn because it meant facing my own shortcomings, stereotypes, the stereotypes held by others, and lastly my unmet expectations. But empathy was pivotal in helping me change my perspective of my situation and it would become crucial in how I saw people as my story unfolded in less and less traditional ways.

That's not to say it wasn't lonely and depressing. I had not yet learned to look for the ways God was preparing me for something greater later on. Instead I was still focused on what I was lacking in the now. I was stuck in the comparison trap watching my friends have the dream that I had been wanting for so long and then also wafting in and out of fear that there really was something wrong with me and that I would remain single until my dying day. A plan I thought was completely flawed. It would take me years to realize that single or married doesn't matter as long as you are listening to the still small voice that is singing to your soul.

For ten years I sat in the sidelines and watched others thrive. In those ten years, college friends married and started families and I made some new single friends. Post-college friends married and started families and I made new single friends again. Those late 20's friends married and started families and I started to ache with being left behind. The ten years of longing and the tenderness I felt as multiple friend groups moved onto the next phase of their lives leaving me single and unattached was nothing small. I had a love/hate relationship with their weddings (I mean, who doesn't love getting dressed up, being fed an amazing meal and dancing the night away?). But I longed to be in their shoes. I longed for more than what I had. Little did I know that God was [still] working on my heart and preparing me in ways I couldn't even begin to see.

So my dreams shifted and became filled with pursuing businesses, being successful, and traveling the world. My focus drifted from that happy home with a large family filled with pattering little feet to being the entrepreneur I knew was itching to get out. God spent years developing and honing me into a different person. One that could navigate difficult situations, handle surprising stresses, manage difficult people, create business plans and oversee budgets, and basically run the show. Surprisingly, these have all been skills I'd need to navigate our adoption experiences. And most importantly, God took those years, when others were getting married and having children and I was not, to show me again and again that He was walking before me, tying loose threads together and providing for me. He took those years to teach me how to hold my hands open and trust him. He taught me to be confident in who He had created me to be, even if that looked so different from what I had expected.

Hear me when I say it wasn't easy or comfortable. It was painful to let go of my expectations of being in a relationship and becoming a mom at young age. Every year on my birthday I felt like I had failed. I was a year older and no closer to my ideal life. It took *years* of feeling like this before it finally dawned on me that my ideal life was whatever one I was living in the song which was being sung to my soul by God. I had to learn contentment *before* the next door opened for me. Why was it so important I learn contentment? Because when your path is the less traveled one, you need to be content on your own path and not be looking at someone else's wondering why that can't be you. Contentment is key to enjoying the blessing of your life. I'm not saying you can't be ambitious-heaven knows I'm more ambitious that most, but my joy comes from contentment with the blessings I have now. This was what I had to learn before I could be a good wife to someone. Before I could be a good mother to children. God knew this and would spend *years* honing my heart.

4

A Quiet Man With A Brave Heart

Anyone who knows my husband will tell you the same things about him. He is quiet, gentle, calming, and yet full of little quips that you'll miss unless you're standing right next to him. He's the person you want to follow in line as you build your burger at the BBQ because he's already planned out the best possible way to build and enjoy it. You will definitely miss out if you don't build it the same way. He's constantly churning around some kind of project in his mind, most likely an invention of sorts, and taking moments here and there to work at whatever problem he has to solve. He's the subtly hot type of guy who rides up on his motorcycle, peeling off his leather jacket, and reveal a polo shirt stretched tight over his lean, muscular body in jeans that are perfectly snug in all the right areas. (Too far? Sorry, I get distracted by him so easily). He will make you the perfect cup of coffee and the perfect cocktail-either of which seem to suddenly appear in your hand. He'll bounce on the trampoline with your kids. He'll pet your dog and cat until they're loyal to him. He cooks better than most people I know, even finishing off my dishes with the perfect seasonings, making people assume I'm the good cook. He's kind, generous, gentle, smart, subtly funny, extremely loyal, selfless to a fault, and so, so quiet.

There's no swagger to his step. He's not full of machismo. There isn't any malice or hate in him. He's quick to forgive, shoulder responsibility, and consistent in unconditional love and forgiveness.

Which is why his story breaks my heart. But it is also what made him the husband and father he is now, and what has allowed him to open his hands to the life God has given us.

Jon grew up in the wilds of outer San Diego. His childhood with his siblings consisted of running through avocado and orange orchards, carving boomerangs out of wood, playing with the band saw in the garage (unbeknownst to his mother), and trying not to injure themselves badly enough to warrant a trip to the emergency room. His community was small, and high school was a grand adventure into the big world. His childhood was safe, wild, and free.

In the first semester of Jon's Christian college experience, while home on a holiday break, he picked up with an old high school flame, which ten months later, resulted in the birth of a son. Those months leading up to the birth were filled with tumultuous, ever-shifting plans for their collective future. Jon and the birth mother's first plan was to place the baby for adoption, and through an online search, found a match. But then they decided against this online match (for reasons Jon can't even remember), and found a local adoption lawyer instead. Through that lawyer they were matched with a lovely couple from the Bay Area - not too far from where Jon was living at the time. The adoptive couple embraced Jon and the birth mother enthusiastically, coming down to Santa Barbara to visit them, and inviting them up and into their world. They reassured Jon and the birth mother that they were making the best decision for their unborn child. Jon remembers sitting with them in church and just feeling the peace of God that this was right.

However, once they revealed their plans to Jon's parents, and his parents realized the seriousness of their plans, his father and step-mother offered to be guardians of the baby. This sent Jon and his girlfriend in a different direction - deciding they would parent. Jon remembers thinking, "If they are going to raise my child, then I should be responsible and raise them myself. This is the right thing to do, and I will make it work." So they decided to make plans to stay together and raise their child. Jon's acute sense of responsibility kicked in and he started to alter his future course to accommodate this new plan - trying again and again to make a plan for the future that would work. But a few months before the birth, some hard truths were revealed, and the wiser course of action was to not raise their child together.

With his heart wrenching in sorrow, Jon let go of the plans he was trying to force. Jon knew what a family should look like. He knew the childhood he had experienced and what he wanted for his child. This left them making the hard decision to place their unborn baby for adoption. Returning to the lawyer and the adoptive couple they had previously selected, they decided once again to make an adoption plan for their unborn baby. He was relieved he no longer needed to force something that wasn't working, but he couldn't shake the deep pain of letting this child go. He couldn't shake the feeling of failing his son.

It sounds so simple and yet the heartbreak is deep and fierce. Through the entire pregnancy Jon wrestled with the best decision for his unborn child and struggled to navigate the complicated situations all by himself. He had at time a very supportive family, a strong group of friends, a college with built-in mentorship programs and counseling services, and yet he went through this all alone. Outside of his parents, he shared his circumstances with only his brother. He didn't feel he could share his situation with others due to preconceived prejudices about unplanned pregnancies, embarrassment, and the unknown future plans. While he felt alone and without wise counsel, he did sense God's hand was orchestrating the bigger picture. He had a deep sense of peace that he was making the right decision when he chose the adoptive couple.

And that adoptive couple - wow. Little did they know that they would set a precedent for Jon (and me) even before we knew what our futures held. When they were first matched with Jon and then birth mother, they began to cover the monthly living expenses and invited them into their lives. But then Jon and the birth mother changed their minds and decided to parent, which I'm sure disappointed the adoptive couple to no end. Here they had waited and waited to be matched with a birth mother, were financially invested, and now being told "Never mind." Then months went by before Jon returned to that couple and asked if they would still be willing to adopt their baby. We'll get to this later, but I cannot believe how gracious this couple was by inviting them into their home, into their lives. This would leave an impression so deep on Jon that 15 years later, when we would be meeting our own birth parents, Jon's openness and graciousness towards them would stem directly from his own experience. His unique perspective allowed him to see our birth parents differently. His own adoptive couple had set the standard of being loving, open, and encouraging.

However, this did not change the weight of what Jon was doing. Prepping for the birth, heading to the hospital when it was time to induce, and holding the sweet boy in his arms - all while knowing he might never see him again - fundamentally changed Jon. He knew deep in his heart he was making the best decision for the future of his child, but he was also experiencing the deep pain of loss before it even happened. Jon's memories of the actual birth and time at the hospital are vague at best. He left school on a Wednesday, drove the four hours south to the hospital, was there for the birth, and then returned to school on Sunday. None of the experiences are clear or in focus, he hardly remembers holding his baby in his arms before passing him along to the adoptive couple. Pictures proved it happened, but his memories have protected his heart. He says he thinks his body was in shock from the weight of his actions. I believe it was God's grace, knowing this could have broken his tender and responsible heart.

No matter how challenging this experience was for him, his choice led us to this path we're on, and it's one I will forever be grateful for. His selflessness, his wisdom, and his ability to let God be in control was a steady hand through the unknowns of our own adoption. It also allowed us to see each birth mother (and each birth father) with compassionate and understanding eyes. Jon knew their pain firsthand. He understood their grief. He also understood the decision they were selflessly making would alter the lives of others around them in the most profound way.

The pain of his decision will never leave him, but neither will the deep peace that it has all been part of God's plan. A plan that lead to our future.

5

I Prefer Rain Showers

We were madly wrapping toilet paper around the girl in the middle, racing the team next to us, and we could hear the laughter of the teams in rooms next door. I was tasked with creating a magnificent headdress for our "bride", while the others struggled to create a flowing skirt and long, long train, convinced that bigger the better would win the competition. Toilet paper was everywhere. Crazed laughter, squeals of, "Hurry, time's almost up", and groans as the strands of paper snapped apart with the slightest movement filled both rooms. And I hated every minute of it. These games were stupid and I'd much rather be spending my Saturday afternoon reading, wine tasting, walking my dog, gardening, honestly *anything* but this.

Did I tell you I hate showers? Not the kind that clean you or that fall from the sky (I love those), the wedding and baby kind. In the seasons of wedding invitations also come shower invitations. Gift in hand, I would arrive at the host's doorstep dreading what lay inside. I would shove down my insecurities about still being single, put on my brave face, and steel my nerves to put up with another round of questions about my love life (lack thereof and *why*) and *what was I doing these days* since I was clearly not doing anything productive by being single. I would competitively create toilet paper wedding gowns and fill out the newly married advice card with something as heartfelt as I could muster. I would suffer through the present opening, exclaiming at the appropriate moments. Was I happy that my friend had found love? Yes, absolutely. Was I also jealous it wasn't me this time? Yes, absolutely.

After the wedding showers came the baby showers. These infernal afternoons spent celebrating the impending arrival of a new precious life. A new life I so desperately wanted in my own. Not that I wanted my friends' babies, but I did consider stealing one a time or two.

Cupcakes were frosted pink, balloons were pink, flowers were pink, everyone seemed to be wearing pink, everything seemed to be pink. It was an onslaught of pink to your eyes. There I was sitting in a room full of fluffily clad married women who were all fawning over the latest baby items in unusually high voices as gifts were painfully, slowly opened one by one. That new diaper pail, this new swaddling set, that darling linen romper with a matching bonnet (okay fine, that was cute). We had just completed decorating onesies for the newborn and were currently trying to resist the temptation to say "baby" lest we have to give up our safety pin attached to our shirts. For the record, I had given up long ago and was now just trying to irk others by saying it as much as possible.

Then there was the conversation. Everything revolved around marriage or children. Complaints of toilet seats left up, socks and shoes perpetually abandoned under the coffee table, mother-in-law dealings, those whose spouses snore and those whose don't, and endless other comparative stories of their married and family life. That was sandwiched between experienced mamas sharing their stories or expectant mamas (of which there were quite a few) planning their stories. Nursery plans, name plans, for heaven's sake preschool plans for their not-yet-born babies. From my outside perspective it seemed like these ladies were doing a lot of complaining about the things I so fervently prayed for. Everyday I would go home to my quiet life and walk my dog. The loud, full, busy lives they were living were what I longed for. Why weren't they shouting their blessings from the top of the pink-wrapped diaper tower instead of complaining?

Now, mind you, most likely they *were* talking about the joys as well as the trials. But from my perspective and from my place of comparison, I only heard the grumbling because I was so caught up in what I was lacking. I had spent so many showers-wedding, baby and even water-miserably discontent because I couldn't see past what I didn't have. I probably missed out on a lot of great stories and tales of joy.

So, I sat there clad in my all-black, one of the few people sipping on the pink cocktail (because most were either breastfeeding or pregnant), thinking about how there was anywhere else I'd rather be. I was completely on the outside of their conversations and experiences. This was no fault of theirs, as they were living their lives to the fullest in their current seasons. I just honestly couldn't relate with my tales of work and dog-parenting. But I was so caught up in myself, that it was just all a very painful reminder of what others were building and I was not. Obviously my dreams from childhood were still there and tender. I longed to build a life with a loving, compassionate spouse and fold tiny baby clothes of my own. I was tired of this cycle of meeting friends and having them marry, have babies and seemingly move on to another life phase. I hit 29 and I felt very, very single.

I had spent 12 years living far away from my family, struggling to separate my desires from the person God was shaping. Struggling trying to find my identity in my work, my single life. Then one day, I weathered another shower in a particularly tender state because I had just ended yet another going-no-where relationship. And it broke me. I went home to my dog and cried about how nothing was going the way I had hoped and planned. It was unfair. I was just as lovely as the next person, why was I in this all-alone place? Why hadn't God given me the desires of my heart? I was mad. I was mad at God and told him so. I used the passages in Psalms liberally as I yelled and ranted at God about the unfairness of this all (quietly, so as not to startle my dog and disturb my roommate). Then my heart calmed. The frustrations I had been carrying around had been laid bare before God. I had nothing else to say. And you know what? He didn't smite me for all my yelling. There were no lightning bolts from the sky, thunderous voices telling me to get in line. There was a quiet small voice in my heart saying there was *a plan already in place*. All this was in preparation for something bigger yet to come. My broken heart trusted this voice.

Then it occurred to me (still small voice again?), that I had a family that loved me. One that supported me no matter what. One that I enjoyed. Why was I living so far away from them? So I picked up my shattered self and moved back home, to be near my family, to be closer to my nieces, to enjoy the friendships of my sisters, and to be closer to my parents and their unending love and support. To relish in the safety and the joy my own family brought me. I was broken, lonely and so frustrated that my life seemed stagnant while others were building theirs.

It was then that I let go of the control of trying to force this life I had imagined. It was then that God met me in a deep, lonely place and promised me a better future than what I could see. It was then that I truly began to see my current life as a blessing instead of a curse. It was then that I truly began to trust God with whatever future he had for me. It was then that my scribbled, jagged self began to take the shape a lot like the one God had planned for me and a lot less like the one I had been trying to become. It was a long year, let's just say that. By the time I hit 30, I was single and for the first time, content with where God was taking me, trusting that the threads He was weaving were better than what I could plan. I couldn't see it yet but trust allowed me peace. A peace like I hadn't known yet.

Then I met Jon.

6

What Best Friends Look Like

J on continued to remain in his college town after graduation where I then met him when I moved back to be near my family. After a few years of being close friends and neighbors, we got married. Me at the ripe "old" age of 33 and him at 30. Lots of people were eager to remind us that my biological clock was ticking and we needed to get on it ASAP, if you know what I mean. But God had other plans for us. We were each so excited to have found a companion eager for adventure, travel, pursuing dreams and passions, that we didn't focus on family building. We instead took ourselves on adventures, traveling as much as we could. We built a floral design business for me and a coffee roasting company for him. We took motorcycle trips, attended cooking schools, took Italian lessons, went to art gallery openings and wine dinners. We got two dogs and a cat. We lived fully and without reserve, building our marriage and companionship over the course of the next four years. We didn't concern ourselves with having children yet, but we also didn't do anything to prevent it either. After years of adventures, starting businesses, taking Italian lessons and cooking classes, and tolerating hundreds of questioning family members about when we were going to start a family, we paused one day and discussed it. We had spent four years loving each other as often and as well as we could, and yet I had not gotten pregnant. With all this lack of prevention, we thought if we were ready for a family God would provide it. God had been preparing our hearts for this moment. We had always known we wanted a family, but had never really talked about the how, the how many, or the timing. But knowing Jon's story, and the journey he took, we were always open to adoption being part of our story too. We just didn't realize it would be the whole story.

Here's the thing. After college, when I was desperately wanting to be married and have children, I wanted to HAVE the children, as in birth them from my body. I longed to know the feelings of carrying a child, experiencing that ritual of motherhood, and the miraculous adventure of feeding the child from your own body. So many of my friends had already passed through this rite of womanly passage and been irrevocably changed by the experience. They claimed it was the worst and best thing to ever happen to them. Not to mention, the end result would be this precious newborn baby-for which I had a deep affinity to. I loved newborn babies. I wanted this for me. I wanted this dreadfully painful and yet exhilarating adventure. The entire experience felt like a secret girl club I wanted to join. Desperately.

But as the years went on without that desire fulfilled and as I grew further away from that early twenty-something person and more into the person God was making me, my heart changed. Believe me when I say I fought it tooth and nail to let go of control and not force anything, but I'd already had enough past experiences relinquishing control to God and then being blessed beyond measure. I still longed for a family, but the "how it comes about" part loosened. I no longer felt this desperation to carry a child, or to have my body change and adapt to birth babies. My focus became more about the baby and less about me.

I relaxed into God's hands and what He had planned for me.

This doesn't mean a part of me didn't cry each month my cycle hit. And it still meant I noticed every pregnant person around me. It felt like everyone was having all the babies while I just wasn't. Just because I was accepting of God's plan didn't mean I enjoyed it. That's the thing about acceptance, it's the releasing of control that precedes joy. I was in the "releasing of control" phase, not the joy phase. You see, before you can truly experience joy, you have to let go of the control that is keeping you from it. You can't enjoy the trip you're on if you're still upset it isn't perfectly 75 degrees like you hoped it would be. You can't find joy in your friendships if they are not living up to the invisible expectations you set for them. You cannot experience joy in your life if you are too busy trying to control all the factors. I spent many, many baby showers as that grumpy guest who brought a gift for the mama, not the baby. I had been so caught up in trying to control the phase of life I was in, that I could not simply enjoy the shower and the friends surrounding me. Those were some of my finer moments, for sure. But now what shifted in me was not just the desire to have a family, that still remained, but how that family was to come about. My perspective shifted drastically as I let go of control.

Like I said (because who doesn't want to keep mentioning sex), for our entire marriage we never prevented pregnancy and we never stopped trying. However, I knew deep down that my body would do what it was capable of and if being pregnant was not something my body could handle, then I wasn't going to press it. I understand and fully respect each person's journey to build a family. It's highly personal and very, very fraught with outside judgment. You will receive no judgment from me for your choices. I just knew for us, for me, I tried all the natural things and then allowed God to show us His plan. We discussed all the other options, but we knew the cost was high and the timing was long and since we weren't rolling in money and we weren't getting younger, we decided we'd rather pursue adoption. The adoption cost rivaled most other options for building a family (have you ever looked into the cost of fertility treatments?), but the odds of coming away with a baby after all was said and done would be a lot higher. So one January, after four years of playing Russian roulette with our bodies and not winning, we decided adoption was our way to build our family.

Five months later, in May, we brought home our first baby girl.

Doesn't that just sound so quick and easy, straightforward and drama free? Well, I think quick was the only thing it was. The five months between making that decision to pursue adoption and bringing home a baby girl were so challenging. Our emotions were all over the place with unexpected challenges, expenses, quick decisions, the stress of the adoption process and the waves of anticipation and joy of what the results of it all would be.

Those months were also filled with a lot of introspection that was certainly character building, but painful in the process. But beneath it all, we knew we were doing the right thing. We were walking in deference to what we believed was God's plan. It might have been challenging to weather those five months, but we had peace that this was where we needed to be.

7

How to Run from the Law

I could see it now, the sweet baby who I'd fed, changed, clothed and cared for over the last nine months and endured sleepless nights together was being taken from me. Her birth mother had worked hard to prove to herself and to the judge that she was fit to be a mother. She had proved to the powers that be that she could feed, change, clothe, and care for this baby whom *I* had held tirelessly in *my* arms. A baby *I* had loved for the last nine months. And I was gutted; Beyond myself. I had spent hours wearing this sweet baby everywhere. Introducing her to my family and friends. Calling her by name. Nights holding her because the only way she'd soothe is if I held her. I already committed my heart and soul to raising her and above all else loving her unconditionally. Now she was being taken back. I could see the Mama Bear in me rising up and protesting, whether or not I believed her birth mother could care for her. I didn't care, this was *my* baby now. No take backs. I'd plan my escape route. Leave for Mexico via the wild, desolate border of Texas. I'd hide deep in the country, sending word to my family via carrier pigeon that I was safe and had changed my identity and to please send money. I would plan it all out.

I promise you I'm not crazy (or *that* crazy), but I did know myself well enough to know that once I committed to something or *someone*-especially a tiny little someone who relied on me for everything-I was in. All in. There was no going back. I could not imagine myself giving back a baby if required. I felt like once that baby was in my arms, I'd flee the country before letting that baby leave my arms-just kidding...maybe. I also had not yet learned to deeply trust God's hands in all this. I think Jon intuitively knew that Mama Bear in me was strong and so was going to guide us towards private adoption instead. Or perhaps he just didn't feel like being a wanted criminal. Either way, we went for private adoption. There are dozens of different avenues for adoption, each one has its strengths and drawbacks. Each its own challenges. *None* are without risks, but we felt like infant adoption was for us.

I had longed to hold that precious, hours-old baby and start the journey together as a family earning my stripes with sleepless nights and 2 AM feedings. I'd always been drawn to newborn babies and had the deep yearning to fill my arms with my own precious newborn. Not all adoption pathways have this as an option. Friends adopting internationally would be matched with a birth mother, but due to the international laws and processing paperwork time, would not meet their baby until well after they were born-most often months later. Or they would be matched with a baby in an orphanage-already months old. I don't know how they didn't just jump on a plane and head over straight away. I didn't have that kind of patience (Don't worry, I learned all my patience when I had four kids under the age of six). Other friends had navigated the complicated layers of the foster system. They had newborns placed in their care, but the entire process was different. There was a continued relationship with the birth parents and foster agency as the birth parents tried to repair their lives and build back up a safe home for their baby. As a foster parent, their job was to care for the baby until the birth mother proved she could care for the child or the court decided that she could not. All these options lead to the same end result-a family being created, being built out of decision and love. Looking back now, this is the first place I should have trusted God's guiding hand and not been so insistent that my desires come to fruition. But this was the beginning our our journey, and I didn't realize I needed to learn that yet.

So I started to make phone calls to agencies that handled infants only. The first I spoke with said one parent had to be a stay-at-home parent. They did not place a baby in a home with two working parents. Living in Central California at the time, it was near impossible to live, let alone pay the steep costs of adoption, without two incomes (unless you have millions stashed away somewhere), and additionally I LOVED what I did. As a third-generation floral designer, I worked whatever hours I set and even took babies with me to errands, client meetings, and wedding installs. Needless to say, that agency was not a good fit for us.

Next, we interviewed a very highly regarded adoption lawyer who spent the entire meeting talking only to Jon and when he finally did acknowledge my presence, asked me what my plan was for my company since I was going to stay home with the baby. Allow me a small digression: I have never once believed that either staying home or working outside the home was "a better choice" for raising children. The best choice for raising children is parents who believe they are making the best choices for their children and their family. If that means leaving a career to raise children, then that is best. If that means working your job to pay for the life you want for your children, then that is best. If that means pausing your career to be at home and then returning in a hybrid manner, that is best. Here's the thing, parents who love their children unconditionally will always be the best choice. We desired children, we were willing to pay exorbitant amounts of money to have these children, we were willingly sacrificing time, freedom, and autonomy to build a family. Whether I stayed home or built a career seemed like a trivial issue in the grand scheme of things. Needless to say, we didn't choose that lawyer either.

There are so many private adoption options that we just knew we could find the one who resonated with us. It felt like it was taking forever to find someone who fit with us. If they were going to help us build our future, we should probably like them. If they were going to represent us before the birth mothers, they should probably believe in us as parents and as a family.

A friend had mentioned a local adoption lawyer and we set up a time to meet right after the New Year. The lawyer suggested meeting at a local wine bar her husband owned. Imagine our surprise when we arrived and found her husband to be someone we had been acquainted with for years through a wine club membership at a local winery. We already loved her husband, so when we met her we connected right away. She was lovely, encouraging and so excited to see us be matched with a birth mother. Our relationship with her was natural and relaxed-nothing like the other conversations we'd previously had. Looking back now, the timing was perfect and we really felt that God had gone before us, giving us the perfect person to help us build our family. From our first meeting we felt she believed in us, loved the life we were going to give a child, and would work tirelessly to help us get there.

Not only that, our lawyer seemed to have great relationships with her birth mothers. Through her stories of previous placements, and the recommendations from other families she'd worked with, we realized she would attempt to build relationships with her birth mothers.

Checking in on them regularly during their pregnancy, meeting them for lunches, and then following up with them after the birth. She cared about her birth mothers and in turn, gained important insight into who they were, discovering pieces of their history and story. Things you would want to know-which we underestimated at first-but now realize where such a gift and still are. If she had relationships with her birth mothers, she could answer questions we might have. I understand these relationships are not always possible due to timing, but she was always attempting to build them. This piece was more important that we realized.

One of the biggest initial fears we had was the fear that the birth mother would change her mind and keep the baby (a lot of people have this fear). This happens and the thought of it was paralyzing. We'd invested all this time and all this money, not to mention subjected ourselves to a bunch of scrutiny (we'll get to that soon), only to have the possibility of having everything fall apart. However, we have learned that the more connected the birth mother feels to the agency or lawyer, the harder it is for them to walk away. As it turns out as well, the more connected the birth mother felt towards us the more likely it would be that she would follow through with her plan. And above all, we now realize that if God had gone before us, then it would work out the way it was supposed to-*for the best*. Our lawyer told us over and over again that if it was going to work out, it would. No amount of fretting in the world that could change the outcome. Of course we didn't listen to her, and agonized over every single thing. We'd learn later that this worry was completely unnecessary. But it would take us four adoptions to figure that out.

So we had this lovely meeting in January with our lawyer at the wine bar and went home elated. We had finally found someone we loved and trusted enough to help us with adoption. We signed the contract, paid the initial fee, and got to work on the mounds of paperwork required to start this non-traditional family.

But let's not gloss over the "paid the initial fee" part quite yet.

8

Money Talk

No one likes talking about money - well, their own money - everyone likes talking about someone else's money. But that's besides the point, Jon and I did not like talking about money to each other or to anyone else. But that was all about to drastically change. Not only would we spend an inordinate amount of time discussing our finances, we'd also start to share them with other people. Something that's horribly embarrassing and humbling all at the same time. I mean, if we wanted to build a family this way, then we *should* be able to pay for it, right? If you can't afford it, then maybe you shouldn't be doing it. Right? *Right?*

Well, no. Not really. If you recall, Jon and I had been married about four years before deciding to pursue adoption. I was just three years new into my entrepreneurial life as a floral designer, so I was still living on the very thin margins of building my business, and Jon worked at a very mediocre paying job. It goes without saying that we were not flush with money. But we *thought* we had enough for adoption. Key word: *thought.*

"How much did it cost?" is a question we knew that loomed loudly in everyone's mind and our first time around we didn't really know the extent of it. As soon as someone hears we have adopted our children, I am often met with "We considered that too." or "We've always wanted to adopt but it was too expensive." I feel like half the world would adopt if it was more accessible and more affordable. There are less expensive ways to go about adopting, like through foster care for example, but those situations are entirely different from what we experienced. They are a different journey completely. Adoption through a representative (agency, lawyer, etc.) whether domestic or international, is expensive. There is no way around this. It's the worst news of the entire process. Every other part of adoption can be beautiful, fun, challenging, life-altering and lovely. The paying for it part? Miserable. So I'm not going to sugarcoat it, but just give you the truth about our experiences and hope that you see the cost was far more than worth it. We learned how to be transparent with our finances, ignoring the social norm of embarrassment. We learned just how much people want to help you build your family. We learned how God provided every step of the way, beyond what we could have planned or imagined (see a theme here?).

Maybe the financial journey was more difficult for us than others, but this part of the adoption process was a huge way God showed us that He was providing for us. We had heard round figures regarding adoption expenses, but we didn't know anyone who could spell it out for us in more exact numbers. We thought we had saved enough money and were prepared, but no we were far from it. We had saved about four months of income that we thought would help us get the process started. We had already looked into financial assistance for adoption, but most of those assistance programs are for international adoption or fostering programs. We didn't find a single one for private adoption.

So, allow me a small tirade of emotion (because this is exactly the internal yelling I felt during our first adoption): the reason adoption is expensive has nothing, *nothing*, to do with the birth mother. Each state has laws in place regarding how much you can help a birth mother with their living expenses. So all, ALL, the other expenses are going market rates. What does that mean? That means there is no regulation on the private sector for how much a representing party (an agency, lawyer, or facilitator) can charge for their services. The price is set by the demand and value it gives to the clients (adoptive families). Sound a lot like a baby market? You're not wrong. If you ever want to hear me go on a political bent about something, this is it. It's atrocious how much adoption professionals and agencies will charge because they can. And people will pay it. People are so desperate to build a family, and have often exhausted all their other options that they are willing to pay for it. Now, some adoption professionals do not exploit the desperate adoptive families although there are a few rotten eggs in every batch giving the industry a bad name. But, and this is a big "but", it is still a free market rate. And often people ask "Can you put a price tag on building a family?"

Yes. Yes you most certainly can. To the tune of a house down payment.

Stop and think about that for a moment. For a very small minority of the population that is nothing. For the rest of us, that is a life-changing figure, a course-altering sum, a *sacrifice-other dreams* amount. But wait! You're doing such an amazing thing adopting an unwanted child! First, hold up on that phrasing and understand that most adoptive children are desperately wanted and loved, but the birth mother has made the infinitely hard decision to not raise the baby, that they are not in the position to do so. If the baby was unwanted and unloved, there are other alternatives. But I am not on that political tangent right now. I am on the money platform.

So back to the cost. A large portion of the expenses is paid to the agency/lawyer/facilitator/consultant for their service of matching you with a birth mother. As other adoptive parents will attest, this process can be as basic as finding a birth mother who wants to place their baby with you called "a match" or more like the relationship we had with our lawyer. This is why being selective with your choice of representative can have such an impact on your experience. Not only are you trusting them to help you build your life, you are paying (a hefty amount) for their services. *You* are the client. If they want to charge market value, then they need to have a level of service that is worth it. That, or we change the policy and regulate how much adoption professionals can charge.

All these things are determined by what state you are living in and adopting in. The following was taken directly from the National Council for Adoption website:

"There is not a uniform adoption code that governs all adoption law in the United States. Each state has its own set of regulations for inter-country adoption, domestic adoption, and post adoption [law regarding the state's follow-up protocol after the adoption is finalized], to determine things like:

- who may arrange an adoption (i.e. attorneys, facilitators, agencies, consultants)
- qualifications to adopt a child domestically (USCIS and other entities also determine this for inter-country adoption)
- home study requirements (these can also vary by agency and some

sending countries have additional requirements)
- interstate or inter-jurisdictional placement requirements and procedures
- when a birth mother may consent to adoption and how long she has to revoke consent
- the rights of unmarried biological fathers in cases where the mother wants to place a child for adoption
- post adoption contact agreement enforceability for infant domestic adoption."

Can you see how much the laws would vary from state to state? And how little control you or the birth mother has over the costs? Each of these items has a cost associated with it that is determined by the market value of the services offer. For example, the home study may require similar documents state to state, and the fees vary widely. It can range from being a couple hundred dollars to several thousands of dollars (a minor budget discrepancy, if one is into budgeting.) This is why it is more important than anything to find a representative (lawyer, agency, consultant, facilitator, etc.) that you trust. One who will advocate for you and help you navigate all the endless expenses. Someone who is upfront with you regarding the costs. We had no idea what to expect until our lawyer made us a list. And then our minds were blown.

Okay emotional tirade and political soapbox over.

So we paid our first payment to our lawyer and expected to wait a bit of time before we were matched with a birth mother. This would be the time we would use to gather more finances, earn a bit more money, and start stashing away the down payment's worth of funds required to pull off this whole family-building thing. But no, ten days later our lawyer called saying she potentially had a match. Cue scrambling for money.

But let's back up.

9

Awkward Family Albums

Remember when we met with our lawyer in that cozy wine bar on a chilly evening the first week of January, signed her contract and paid her fees. After that she went off to find us a birth mother and we went off to start all the required processes for adoption. Imagine our surprise when she called about a week later saying she had a potential birth mother for us, twins of all things, being born in March, in Florida. (Quick reminder: we were in California, a mere 2,600 miles away). We were thrilled, *thrilled*, to have an option so quickly. Only they would be born in six weeks. *Of course* we were interested, I mean we were riding the high of the excitement of this journey. I didn't even stop to think about how we'd need to come up with all the money to fund this adoption, not to mention the fees for two states within six weeks. But I just had this panicky feeling that if we said no we wouldn't be matched again anytime soon-or at all-and we'd lose our opportunity.

And this is what I'll tell you. That was stupid. Don't listen to that fear. God knew our life. He knew I had dozens of floral design commitments I couldn't miss. He knew Jon's job wasn't flexible enough to drop everything and fly to Florida for an extended stay, rearranging all our schedules at the last minute. And don't even get me started on caring and managing twins after birth. Not to mention we couldn't afford it. God knew we couldn't handle the expenses, let alone the logistics, which we wouldn't be able to make work. So when I slowed down enough to listen to that still small voice guiding us, we had a peace about letting it go. We took a big breath and said no to that opportunity, nervously trusting God that he had another plan. If I could emphasize anything to any of you considering adoption-don't panic, the right situation is out there for you and you don't have to jump at the first one.

It was a good thing we said no because not even a week later, another possibility arose. I remember our lawyer called me on a *Wednesday*, about ten days after meeting her for the first time, and said there was a birth mother looking for a family. Through one of our lawyer's colleagues (adoption lawyers will often network with others to build their cache of available birth mothers and adoptive families), our lawyer had heard about a birth mother who was down in the Los Angeles area. She thought we may want to consider this situation since the birth mother was being presented with adoptive family options on *Monday*. She was wondering if we'd like the opportunity to present as well. Quick side note: being "presented" means your information is put in front of the birth mother for consideration. This was easy to say yes to. It was close, so no travel expenses were needed. She wasn't due until late spring, so there was lots of time to collect our finances and prep. We just felt like this was a good situation for us. We were high on the excitement of potentially becoming parents soon-and then all the logistics hit.

So. Many. Logistics. It was all-consuming, overwhelming and so unexpected to us. We knew adopting would cost money (a quick internet search will tell you that). We knew we'd have to fill out paperwork. But we did not know that we'd have to bare our souls to everyone and the state *and* jump through hoops to prove we'd be acceptable and qualified parents. Over the course of the next few months, we had to procure letters of recommendations from people we'd known for years, get fingerprinted, and subject ourselves to a state analysis of our living situation, just to name a few. But before our lawyer could even present us to that birth mother as potential adoptive parents, we had to assemble a portfolio for her. We had to scramble to put together a visual portfolio and we had six days to do it. I've never been a scrapbooker, so it's not as though I had organized picture files ready to go. I was pulling a visual representation of our life together in one weekend hoping it would convince this sweet birth mother that we'd be good parents for her unborn baby. No pressure. No pressure at all.

We certainly didn't understand the whole process and it seemed there were so many pieces happening at once. In private adoption the lawyer or agency has a network of birth mothers through their contacts who are interested in making an adoption plan for their unborn child. As potential adoptive parents, we were to fill out an application for our lawyer and create a portfolio explaining our lives. Our lawyer would then present her birth mothers with our and other adoptive couples' portfolios. I like to describe these portfolios as very awkward family photo albums where everything about us and our lives was distilled into a short photo album and then described by long, detailed captions that help the birth mother get an idea of who we are and what kind of life we lead. For example, there might be a picture of Jon on his motorcycle with the caption that reads, "Jon likes to take motorcycle rides in his spare time", or a picture of me surrounded by buckets of flowers underneath which says, "Anna is a wedding floral designer with a home studio and a lovely team composed of mostly her family" (those may or may not have been the exact captions). The portfolio also has a few pages that describe our family values and what life we can offer a child. It is basically a marketing booklet that will be presented alongside other adoptive families' portfolios, and may the best family win! Just kidding, sort of.

It was during this scrambling that it dawned on me. No matter how beautifully I laid out our portfolio; no matter how attractive we made our lives to this birth mother; no matter how many perfect pictures and captions I could assemble together, the bottom line was that if this baby was destined by God for our arms, that would be it. No amount of finesse would alter his plan. So we put our best selves forward, swallowed the embarrassment of awkward captions and uncomfortable marketing of ourselves, and passed the book off to our lawyer with a prayer. My prayer was that if this was God's plan, it would be clear to us.

At the same time we created our portfolio, we filled out an application answering dozens of questions about preferences that would help guide our lawyer into finding the best birth mother match for us. Being honest while filling out this application was crucial but also sobering. Jon and I had to discuss things we've never considered, nor would ever need to consider if we were having a biological child. We had to examine our hearts and make sure we weren't answering out of guilt. Filling out this application was actually stressful and confusing. But having our lawyer get to know us and be able to answer personal questions about us on our behalf was extremely important. While she represented a dozen or so adoptive families, she also truly cared that we were a good match with the birth mother. She wanted to find a birth mother that was excited about our life and the way we were living it–who would feel relieved to place their child with us. But that also meant we had to reflect on and answer questions that were vulnerable and revealing about who were and what we wanted for our life.

It started out with simple things, like do you want a boy or a girl? Or how about twins? These were easily answered for us (*yes* to everything). Would you consider other races? Initially this felt a little political, until we really considered what this meant. We thought through our extended family dynamics and what races were already present as well as what prejudices existed (let's be real, everyone has THAT uncle). We considered the community we lived in. We thought through our circles of friends. Our cultural practices. Would they feel isolated? If they were a person of color, would they lose their heritage being adopted into our white family or could we incorporate new traditions and practices? Being a very white female (and by that I mean deathly pale, vampire-like in coloring), we wanted to make sure any baby we brought home of any race would not feel alone in their skin. We wanted to make sure they were exposed to their heritage and cultural practices. Fortunately for us, we have many friends with mixed race marriages, adopted family members of different ethnicities, and a community that was super supportive.

Then the application took a nosedive into the deepest unspoken fears of our hearts. Would you consider a baby that has known congenital anomalies? If so, check the boxes of which you would consider-and then there's a list of every possible anomaly-deaf, blind, fetal anomalies, neurological congenital disorders, etc. The list was thorough and something we had never discussed. We had to examine our hearts. Consider all the consequences of our decision. We had to consider our limits both financially and physically. And then we had to re-examine any pre-conceived notions we had been unknowingly carrying around. We had to come face to face with some dark truths about us. Would we only consider a "perfect" child? Would we reject one less than that? Does anyone want to face these questions? Each precious birth mother making a plan for their unborn baby, trying to be as responsible as she could and give her child a life she could not provide, did not want to deliver a baby with an anomaly only to have the adoptive parents walk away. Can you imagine the heartbreak? Can you imagine the rejection the birth mother would feel?

We were asked to consider drug and alcohol exposure and which drugs, if any, we were willing to consider. This was an educational experience for us as we researched and consulted with wise, experienced friends, about which drugs had long-term consequences, what they were, and if it mattered to us. We had to consider if we could afford both the time and money it would take to remain in hospital while the baby detoxed and recovered–which could be weeks, even months.

It was best Jon and I examined our hearts and knew exactly what we could handle and what we could not. We had to examine our motives, our desires, and pray specifically about what we were designed to handle as parents. We rested in the truth (and released ourselves from guilt) that if we said "no" to some questions, someone else was saying "yes". This is the beautiful thing. There are so many families wanting to adopt that there are enough homes for all the babies. And in each situation, each adoptive family has different capacities and limits. That meant, no matter how we were to answer these questions, God had a plan for all the unborn babies. We could release ourselves from the guilt of not saying yes to everything. He had created our family a certain way and whatever baby was placed in our arms would be just right for us and our family.

Our lawyer did the best she could to guide us through the process of adoption and prepare us for what was ahead, but her job was to find a birth mother for us, not hold our hand while we anxiously processed all the emotions that arose with the application or the potential matches. We had very few contacts who had adopted and could explain some of the more confusing and nuanced parts of adoption. Fortunately for us, Jon's brother and sister-in-law had already walked this road so they were an amazing resource. They answered so many of those uncomfortable questions we could hardly bring ourselves to ask. Questions that suddenly we didn't even know we had until we were filling out the adoption application and building our portfolio. We realized that not many people had resources like them, and most felt lost in the process. We came to the conclusion that whatever journey we took with each child, we would be an open book and resource for others considering adoption. We promised ourselves that we would not let others feel so lost and confused the way we did that first time (hence this book).

Creating the portfolio and filling out the application had a way of stripping away any pretenses we had. We might have wanted to appear a certain way-open to any situation, financially able to handle all the options, happy with any outcome-but that would have been a lie and could have deeply affected our lives and the life of our unborn baby. If we lied about what we were capable of handling now, what would happen when that lie came into the light? Would we resent the innocent child who deserved a family that could care and wanted to care for them? If we weren't honest about our finances, would we end up having to pull out of an adoption because we had misled our lawyer and the birth mother into believing we could handle more than we could? The thing is, no matter how hard those questions were to answer, those questions forced us to be honest with ourselves. There were moments when we looked at each other, embarrassed to admit our shortcomings, but realized in our honesty we were building a stronger marriage and future family. Those questions forced us to really trust that God *knew* us and had designed for us the right situation.

10

Arranged Marriage

So Monday morning our lawyer and her colleague presented our hastily assembled, awkward photo album portfolio to the birth mother alongside the others. And then we waited. Two nerve-rattling days we waited to hear if the birth mother had selected us. I distinctly remember the feeling of our future being completely outside of our control, of hardly being able to sleep because this decision would alter our lives...or not. We'd either be on a crash course towards starting a family or we'd be back to square one. We didn't tell a single soul what was going down for fear it wasn't going to happen.

Then our lawyer called. The birth mother had chosen us. We felt in awe, like we were sleep-walking through a dream, like perhaps this wasn't real. We were honored to be selected. I've never been pregnant, but I assume it's a similar moment to finding out you're pregnant. We found ourselves walking around in a daze-in a surreal state-the slow understanding seeping into our minds that our lives would never be the same again.

We waded our way through this seemingly innocent, yet revealing application in record time. We had about five days to fill out the application and build our portfolio so our lawyer could present us to the birth mother in the timeline her colleague had created-we were a last minute addition to the adoptive parents she was going to present to the birth mother. But this just felt right to us. Unlike the twins from Florida, we had peace about this. But this also meant we had to scramble and come up with a second match fee. A lot of adoption lawyers work together in networks and will pool their birth mothers and clients as supply and demand fluctuates to help make better matches more quickly. This means you might pay the match fee twice (we have for two of our adoptions). Or you might pay a marketing fee to be added to a website where birth mothers can review your portfolio. For example, maybe you have signed with a lawyer but she has another lawyer friend with a bunch of birth mothers right now. Your lawyer might suggest one of those birth mothers as a good match for you, but if you are matched with that birth mother, you now pay your lawyers' colleague their match fee as well. Of course they would run this by you, but this would double your adoption professional fees. So one house down payment becomes two, or three months of savings becomes six, or something equally as scary.

But back to that second match fee. A sacrificial amount of money-why would we even consider working with a third party if we didn't have the extra money to spare on a second match fee? Well, in short, because we didn't know better. We barely understood how the adoption world worked. We asked our lawyer for the breakdown of expenses for her process and thought we could handle the low end of them, which would equate to about three months of living expenses for us. We were naively hopeful that the amount wouldn't creep up. But then we were told about this birth mother in Los Angeles, and all our emotions flew up in our faces at the idea of holding a precious newborn come May. We told ourselves we could do this. We could figure out the money which was projected to be about half of Jon's yearly salary. If anything, I'm the eternal optimist of "I can figure this out." So we nervously clutched the second largest check we'd ever written in our lives and drove in a nervous silence to meet her. Our potential birth mother. The woman who may be carrying our child. It wasn't scary at all.

We arranged to meet our lawyer, her colleague, and the birth mother at a non-description restaurant. This meeting was to confirm that yes, we did want to be matched with the birth mother, to sign the contract, and pay the match fee to our lawyer's colleague. We told no one we were going. We still hadn't told anyone we had been matched. We had barely mentioned to our family that we were starting the adoption process. Friday morning, exactly one week after learning about this birth mother, we took a very tension-filled, two-hour drive to the meeting, reassuring ourselves that no matter what transpired that day, we'd be okay.

We met and well… it was like the most awkward blind date we'd ever experienced, and I've had my fair share of really weird blind dates. We sat across the table in a restaurant and shyly assessed each other. She was a striking girl with long dark hair, beautiful big blue eyes, and full pink lips that she was nervously biting. Her large eyes were taking us in as we approached. Our lawyer and her colleague did most of the talking, but I wanted to ask her *all* the questions. I wanted to know about her family. About her life. What she liked. What dreams she had. She seemed equally interested in us. However, at the time I didn't know that initiating those questions and seeing her as a person (not just a means to get a baby), would be crucial to understanding a bit about our future child. In all our other experiences we would have very, very little interaction with each birth mother, barely a chance to get to know them at all. I didn't pelt her with questions at that lunch, and fortunately we did get to know this sweet woman in the months leading up to our first born's birth. But we learned that during those first meetings, we needed to take our time and get to know the birth mothers as best we could because it might be the only chance we'd have. In one of our experiences, this initial meeting would be the only time we ever spoke to the birth mother outside of the hospital. So maybe this meeting was less like a blind date and more like a high pressure arranged marriage introduction. But no matter, we weathered it like champs. We didn't let her see how crazy we actually were. Turns out we loved the birth mother and she loved us. We signed the paperwork, handed over our massive check, and walked away from that meeting just *knowing* it was right. To say our faith grew that evening is an understatement. We drove home in awe of how God had gone before us and provided for us in a way that was so unexpected and so good.

Then the weight of what just transpired hit us. We would be parents in four short months. All the what-ifs started. The fears started to creep in. The reality of the amount of money we just committed to hit us. All the unknowns of what we had just contractually obligated ourselves to flooded our minds. We began a journey where we really truly learned how to relinquish control and know deep in our hearts that God had a plan for us. He already knew the whole story and would walk with us. It had been two weeks since we first met our lawyer and the next four months were some of the scariest, most beautiful months we would ever experience.

11

How to Have Control

I want to go back to one thing I just glossed over, but was an emotional battlefield each time we adopted a child: how we decided this was a good match for us. After all, we only had one blind date to really assess the situation. Was it based on factual information about the birth mother? Was it based on the needed expenses? Was it purely a gut feeling? As I mentioned previously, we had been asked about the twins in Florida, which we turned down. And in-between our other adoptions we would be asked to consider other opportunities, but we would turn those down as well. In all honesty, the only birth mothers we chose to be presented to were the ones who selected us. How is that possible? Everyone knows someone who has been waiting years to adopt with failed opportunity after failed opportunity disappointing them.

I think in independent adoption, the amount of work which the lawyer or agency puts into each birth mother relationship directly relates to how successful those matches will be. Every representative is different, but one thing they all try to do is get to know their birth mothers. They have them fill out an intake form with medical history, personal history such as likes and dislikes (for example, their favorite color and favorite food), valuable insights regarding potentially crucial information (such as any record of diabetes in the family), their current living situation and their essential budget (including food, shelter, transportation, and communication). That way, they can better support them through the process, help answer their questions, and hopefully keep a connection with them strong enough to help them really understand that, while making an adoption plan is hard, it is a huge blessing for the adoptive families.

I know I referenced this earlier, but to be "matched" with a birth mother means they learn about you and you learn about them and then they select you for their child. Of course the information you give to your representative is meant to reveal as much as possible about you and your life so that the birth mother feels comfortable placing a baby with you, hence our awkward family photo album portfolio. Most of the information requested by your representative is actually required by law, but we'll get to that later. On the other hand, the information the birth mother gives to the lawyer or agency is not legally required, and therefore, not as forthcoming and varies a lot from individual to individual. There are not a lot of requirements on what the birth mother needs to reveal, so what they divulge is up to their discretion. The birth mother is coming from a place where they need to make a better plan for their child than what they can provide. This might be out of a concern for safety, financial distress, family conflict, or general wisdom that they are not the best option for raising their child. This may mean some of their story is sensitive and will not be revealed. Or perhaps they are embarrassed and don't want to share. The lawyers and agencies do their best to get crucial information (like medical history) from each birth mother, but sometimes the information is vague.

While our lawyer did share some details with us from these forms before we were presented, so that we could decide if each match was a good match for us (similar to the way the birth mothers would review our portfolios), the sensitive information was kept private until a baby was placed with us. Then the forms would be passed along to us as this was now part of the child's story. We valued, and still value, these forms so much because they are a link to the history of each of our children. They remain the only link we have to each child's history. But even before we had the sensitive information, we would take 24 hours and pray through each birth mother before opting to be presented to them. We would weigh the details we did have and the budgets we had been provided. We would wait quietly before God for the sense of peace He would provide. Peace amidst all the angst, worry, fears, and stresses.

I think it's important to be forthcoming and say that so many questions we had went unanswered in all our situations. Either no one had the answers or we just weren't going to get an answer. Often we felt like we were going in blind, committing to a life-changing event without knowing all the facts. In our first scenario, we asked about the birth mother and were given some cursory facts about her (hair color, height, nationality, etc.), some vague pregnancy details (she was having a girl), and a general budget of her expenses. But that was it. We didn't see a family medical history chart, or a list of her personality traits and interests, or important details about her living expenses, such as due dates for bills that we'd be expected to cover for the next six months. We prayed over these non-details and submitted our portfolio. Then, when we were selected by her, we received more detailed personal information regarding her medical history, family history, and such. But both this time and with the others, it wasn't very exhaustive. So when we did meet with her, we had a better picture of who she was, but not by much. Meeting with her was just to solidify that we'd want to go forward with this. So again, we were making a life-altering decision not based on all the facts, but on the very vague details we had been provided, and our intuition. I'd say it was about 20% details and 80% intuition. Not scary at all, right?

This was the first test of our willingness to let go of control and trust instead. Later we would learn this was the hardest decision we would make when agreeing to a match because it meant we were allowing this unknown birth mother's story to become our own future without knowing all the things. The child we raise would be completely foreign to us. They would not have the genes we were familiar with-uncle Bob's sense of humor, Grandma Becky's zest for life, my eyes. They would be like a small bud beginning to unfurl, with no expectations or indications of what they would become when they fully blossomed. It was (and still is) incredibly scary to watch them unfurl their petals and not know what is ahead. But it has also been one of the most freeing parental experiences, because we have *No. Expectations. None.* We simply don't know who they will become and so we get to hold them with our hands open, our eyes glued, waiting for them to unfurl and become something beautiful.

Watching one child love art and drawing, and then knowing her birth mother did too, has been a gift to us as parents. Seeing the natural math brain emerge in another child, and know their birth father was also highly intelligent was beautiful to experience. We did not have thorough information for each child and that, at first, caused great fear. What were we getting ourselves into? What about all those application questions that were now seared into our minds? In some of our adoptions, we didn't have a full medical history and so we had no idea if the baby would be born with a life-changing anomaly. These fears were huge. I definitely had panic dreams where I imagined four noses and 27 toes on our newborn babies and then woke up all sweaty, having to talk myself off the ledge.

We had to face the fears that surrounded us and surrender our thoughts each time. We had let go of control every time. *Every single time.* It would not get easier with each adoption. Our trust would increase each time, but the fears would still be there. We had to acknowledge that whether we had all the baby's history or not, God was going to walk with us as we raised each child. Each child we were given would be a mystery and an amazing blessing of discovery which would be a gift to us and the child. By our fourth adoption, we had practiced this relinquishment enough that we were able to say yes to an adoption with very little information (due to the circumstances) and *mostly* not freak out in fear. After six years and four adoptions we would truly believe and understand in our small finite minds that God's hand was over each birth mother that chose us and over each baby that was placed in our arms.

12

Not Ours Anyway

"*E*veryone to whom much was given, of him much will be required, and from him to whom they entrusted much, they will demand the more." *(Luke 12:48)*

What if we considered this charge beyond the traditional interpretation of finances? What if the "much you were given" was actually your children? What if the much Jon and I were given was actually the precious babies we'd been entrusted with? It makes you reconsider all your fears, complaints, and frustrations. Suddenly, our focus shifts from money troubles to tangible, living, breathing, beings that are relying on us to provide for them, guide them, and lead them into strong futures.

So we drove home from our meeting with our first birth mother on cloud nine. Me sitting in the passenger seat searching online for all the baby things that I never could bring myself to search before, the pain of not having children had been, well, too painful, to indulge in browsing all the cute items. It's one of the main reasons I would bring gift certificates for massages and other gifts for the mother to a baby shower. I just couldn't browse all the tiny things without my heart breaking. And now *finally* it was my turn. I gleefully showed Jon all the cool modern baby items we could have, my heart soaring in my chest. Hardly able to believe it was finally our turn to plan for the impending arrival of a tiny being.

Then we spiraled. Freaking out about all the unknowns and the task list ahead of us (three hours in the car can really do a number on your psyche). By the time we arrived home the surreal had worn off and the buying baby clothes and prepping a nursery were the last things on our minds. Honestly, we still held our breath not sure if this would come together or not. We spent the next five months teetering on the edge of ecstatically hopeful and too afraid to get excited. We were forced to learn how to hold our hands open to whatever transpired. This happened with each child. We'd match with their birth mothers, be elated, then spend the entire pregnancy holding our breaths, vacillating between the excitement of a new baby and the fear the birth mother would change their mind. Once we said yes to a match we were already in so deep emotionally and financially that the fall out would be substantial should the birth mother reconsider her options.

Once we agreed to a birth mother, we would be responsible for her living expenses until six weeks after the baby was born. They would be relying on us to take care of them, to provide for them. What are these birth mother expenses? They are the most widely varying expenses because it depends on so many different factors, but usually it's their monthly living expenses. No matter how you go about private adoption, whomever represents you wants to have funds on hand to provide for the birth mother's pregnancy and living expenses. You will never give money directly to a birth mother, it is actually prohibited by law so it can not be construed as "paying for a baby."

a) It is a misdemeanor for any person or agency to offer to pay money or anything of value, or to pay money or anything of value to a parent for the placement for adoption, for the consent to an adoption, or for cooperation in the completion of an adoption of his child.

However, each birth mother has living expenses that are determined by the agency or lawyer and you are asked to cover them. These expenses are rent, car payments, cell phone bills, utilities, food - pretty much everything outside of discretionary spending and sometime even that too. Most often the expenses will be covered from the moment the birth mother starts working with an agency/lawyer until six weeks after the baby is born, as is California law where we were adopting. But, it does vary by state with similar undertones dictating your level of financial commitment to the birth mother. That means, if the birth mother begins the process with the agency when she is five months pregnant, but she is not matched with adoptive parents closer to her due date, then the adoptive parents will repay the agency all previous expenses the agency incurred. Not only that, all the expenses going forward until six weeks after the baby is born will be covered by the adoptive parents. Usually these amounts are requested in lump sums by your representative and kept in an escrow account to be dispersed by them to the birth mother as needed. For example, she would be given enough to cover her monthly bills before the rent is due. Obviously, living expenses vary by area, so these expenses do as well. These are also not refunded should the birth mother change their mind and decide to keep their baby.

The first time we adopted, we didn't know much about these expenses and barely understood how it worked. We had asked our lawyer for a projected amount for birth mother expenses, which she provided and it proved to be about the same as our own monthly budget. But the sum could change and did change, as we discovered. Birth mother living situations can also change which will directly affect their monthly expenses. Our birth mother's living situation changed quite a few times in those four months and so the budget increased with each change.

For us, the birth mother's expenses were initially one of the harder expenses for us emotionally. In a couple of our adoptions, the birth mother's living expenses were higher than our own tightly regulated monthly budgeted expenses. Once these funds were disbursed to cover her expenses, we would not recoup them, even if the adoption fell through. So, it felt so hard to send this money off, when we personally weren't even spending that much and scraping by so we could afford these adoptions. But, after a couple times of doling out living expenses, I started to look on them as a gift-a gift with which I could bless each birth mother. They had selflessly chosen the option of adoption. They had chosen the harder route, one that would involve their own bodily discomfort and emotional distress not only during the pregnancy, but a long time after as they recovered. The least I could do was help them be comfortable and survive the months of pregnancy and recovery.

It makes me sound like I was a hardhearted scrooge, and let's be honest maybe I was, but this is one of the areas God used to soften and change my heart. I began to let go of our money and really understand that He was in control of our finances and He was using us and what little we had to help change someone's course of life just as they were altering ours. By the fourth child, I had finally learned to give willingly and even excitedly, hoping that whatever we could provide for the birth mother would give her a hand up, perhaps help change her future. Even if she changed her mind and decided to raise the baby herself, we would have helped her during a tough time. And let's be honest, it wasn't our money in the first place. It all belonged to God and we were just managers of what He had given us. He had given us these finances so that we could give them to these birth mothers and pay for these adoptions. In exchange, we would be given one of the biggest responsibilities of our lives, way beyond financial management, we'd be asked to raise and care for these children.

But let's be real for a moment. We did not have the money to do this the first time around. We were initially given a range by our lawyer that would require us to budget close to one quarter of our annual income for our first adoption and we were going to leverage everything we had to do this. Then after we agreed to match with this birth mother in Los Angeles, our fees suddenly spiked. Now we were looking at closer to one third or one half of Jon's yearly salary. This was an insane amount of "extra" money to us. We even took out a small personal loan to help cover the costs. While all our friends were buying houses and starting their more traditional life pathways, we were focused on making ends meet to cover these expenses. Any ideals we had about purchasing our first home or taking an extra trip, were quickly squashed by the insane (to us) amount of money we were about to spend.

We had struggled with the idea of asking friends and family to help us. We really truly didn't think we should ask. We had made the choice to adopt and so we felt like we needed to pay for it on our own. Our friends were already living tight with their own financial struggles and their own endless expenses. Besides, we had already painted the perfect picture of our lives-one full of international travel, weekends away, dinner parties, and motorcycle adventures. To all of our external audiences (I'm looking at you, social media), it would appear we were financially set. That we were blessed with deep pockets. And sure, if you had told us when we were first married that we should start saving now for what would eventually add up to two years worth of income in adoption expenses, maybe we would have taken fewer trips. But we had no idea this would be our future. We also had no idea just how much it would cost when all was said and done. So we took all the money we had saved, that would have become a down payment for a house, and earmarked it "adoption."

But it still wasn't enough. And after a couple months of expenses in our first adoption we humbled ourselves and asked for help. In our society, finances are private, embarrassing even. It's shocking to hear someone mention exactly how much money they have or how much money they need. But we felt we needed to be transparent. We felt we needed to let people know we were striving to make this work with everything we had and we were still coming up short. Yes, we could have waited and saved more until we had enough to cover the expenses ourselves (and in future adoptions we would), but this first time around we truly didn't know the extent of the costs. By the time we had committed to both our lawyer, her colleague, and the birth mother we were caught off guard and would stand to lose a lot of money if we walked away from this match. So we asked for help. It was humbling, embarrassing, and felt unjust.

I want to be fully transparent with you now. I deeply felt the unfairness of it all. What had Jon and I done to deserve this? All we had wanted to do was start a family, and now not only would we have to pay large sums to do so, but we would have to ask for help to do it. It hurt to think about how our journey was so seemingly different from everyone else's. How my roommates from college had already effortlessly birthed their children, bought their family homes, and now were in the season of school plays and sporting events. Meanwhile Jon and I had to admit to our world that we didn't have enough money to bring home the one baby that was being given to us. I was mad and frustrated with God. I was angry that this was the journey we were on. Truthfully, I was more angry for Jon's sake than my own. He'd worked so hard to bring in the money we needed for this and he had already suffered through his own storms. Why couldn't it be easy and smooth sailing for him at least? Why was God allowing all this discomfort and embarrassment? Hadn't Jon been through enough already? But see, that's part of the story we needed. We needed to see just how much we needed other people, our village.

And you know what? Our village showed up. They met us and provided. We put together a simple fundraising page that spelled out exactly what we needed and nervously posted it on social media. We were open about the costs of specific processes, like the home study charges and the monthly birth mother expenses. We laid out carefully that we had already been matched with a birth mother and didn't want to walk away from her just because we couldn't come up with the finances to cover all the expenses. We were genuine, honest, and humble with our request, not expecting a huge response. We were surprised so many people respond with encouraging notes and generous gifts. High school friends we hadn't seen in years, college roommates, acquaintances from my wedding work, coworkers of Jon's. Most friends simply donated $40 and wished us the best. But you know what? That $40 multiplied across 200 people, and suddenly, we had bridged the gap we needed.

We had one couple call and generously, oh-so-generously, gift us with part of their inheritance from the recent passing of a family member. It was beyond generous. I distinctly remember sitting in my sun-drenched back yard in early spring receiving her call. She was saying how it had been laid on their hearts to help us. How they wanted to help us start our family. As she talked I was aware of the sun on my back, the weight being lifted off my shoulders, and the awareness that

God was providing and laying out a pathway before us even when we couldn't see it. We had seen only our shortcomings of thinking, "If only we hadn't traveled as much. If only we hadn't lived in that one town-home in Santa Barbara. If only I hadn't become self-employed with no steady income."

What we underestimated was our community's willingness to help. They wanted to take their $40 (or in my friend's case, a lot lot more) and gift it to us. We weren't twisting any arms or asking for any favors. They believed in what we were doing and saw the bigger picture. They wanted us to have a family. They wanted the unborn child to have a loving, devoted, and unconditional family. Our willingness to be transparent with our financial situation and reveal our adoption plans actually became a blessing to others. We would have missed all this had we not been willing to ask for help, be transparent, and humble ourselves in our need. We would have missed seeing how God provided for us now *and* showed us how in the future we can do the same for others. We realized that this unborn child was going to be a gift beyond us. We then realized that our adoption (and the adoptions yet to come) had a bigger purpose beyond building a family. Our story would be a witness to God's provision, our faith and His blessings.

13

Laying Naked

I was madly dashing around our tiny two-bedroom, one-bath cottage tidying every surface I could see. Not that there was anything left to tidy, my nerves were just making me turn about the room again in hopes they'd settle. I had just folded my underwear and relocated the cleaning products up to a high shelf in the laundry room. Earlier I had furiously fluffed the couch pillows, threatening both man and dog that their lives would be forfeit if they did sit on them. We had organized the pantry, mopped the floors, cleaned the garage, and organized the pantry again. The dog had been groomed, the garden had been weeded, and Jon and I had prepped for our test the best we could, without actually knowing what test we were taking. I was sweating and trying not to show it. What if we failed? What if they denied us?

This was the culmination of weeks of hard work as we assembled all our paperwork for the home study. After we truly committed to our birth mother financially (and paid those match fees), we jumped right into working on the needed documents to make this adoption legal. To say it is a thorough process would be an understatement. This home study was the state's way of making sure we were not creeps who cannot and should not care for children. This is also their way of intimidating us as they pried through our history, asked us all sorts of questions we hadn't considered, and opened all the cupboards in our house to see what we were hiding. Oh, that's not the purpose of it? Well that's what it felt like to us. We didn't understand the extent of the home study process when it was mentioned to us by our lawyer. She said we'd need to complete a home study through a third party agency and we thought that meant some questions about if we had a crib or a safe car seat. We did not realize that this was an actual in-depth analysis into our lives, current living situation, and our future selves as parents. Listen, a home loan application is nothing compared to this home study.

Now don't get me wrong, I completely understand why these checks and safeguards are in place. To be the caregiver for a child is a serious responsibility and, at least in California, the state will compensate you for the time and effort you put into caring for a foster child. This compensation, of course, attracts all sorts of individuals. Individuals who are safe, loving, sacrificial, and have the child's best interest in mind....and those that are, well, none of those things. Those unsavory individuals are sadly in it for the compensation only. So this home study process is meant to weed out those repugnant individuals who make the process that much harder for the rest of us. But it did feel wrong to us the first time around that we would be scrutinized so heavily-not only were we not being compensated for caring for this child we would adopt we were also *paying* to do this.

We honestly felt like we were lying naked before the social worker. Here's our salary records and copies of our tax returns. Here's our weight, height, and analysis of our health condition-wait, you actually need us to go get physicals? Okay, here are the doctor's reports stating the quality of our health and stress levels. (By the way, if you're wondering how we scored, Jon was near perfect. Are we surprised? Not at all.) Here are our fingerprints. Here are our criminal background checks and, oh, our driving records. The physical wasn't enough? We need tuberculosis tests? Here are our tuberculosis test results. Here is the medical history of our extended family. Here is an exhaustive explanation of why we want to adopt. Here are five letters of recommendations from friends who have known us for more than three years and who can attest to our capability of potentially being parents. Here is a 2,367 page biography of each of us. Okay, the last one might be a lie, but the rest were actually required and surprise, surprise, none were free. You thought we'd be out picking car seats and strollers? No, our days off were spent chasing down forms that needed completing.

So I finished racing around, sweating through my shirt, pulling the freshly made cookies out of the oven (because first impressions, right?) just as the social worker knocked on the door. She was lovely as she interviewed both of us, first together then separately, checking our answers against each other's. She toured our home, faithfully, opening cupboards, peering in drawers (good thing I folded that underwear), and asking where we kept toxic cleaners and medicines. She asked us if we had any guns or pools (because those are the same). She was creating an *analysis of the quality of our marriage* (the section is literally titled that), of our lifestyle, finances, and mental health. And she literally wrote up an analysis of our home and if she would recommend it as a safe place for an adopted child. And then, *and then*, we had to provide our philosophy of parenting. We actually had to write out what method of discipline we'd use in the future with the baby who hadn't even been born yet.

Now anyone who is a parent will laugh at all the times they thought they'd never be "that parent" with their discipline style. Of course we'd never raise our voice, turn on a device, or feed our child chicken nuggets. *We* will not be that kind of parents. And now we laugh at ourselves. We had no clue what we were getting into. We had no clue what childhood behaviors would trigger our darker sides, making parenting nearly impossible. We had no idea what type of personality we'd be up against with each child (does anyone ever really know?) So looking back, and I'm sure if I was to reread our answers, I'd laugh at our idealistic and completely unrealistic responses.

After this interview and home study process, I feel like we could have obtained the highest level of top secret clearance. Actually, I think this home study might be more exhaustive than that. Did I mention we paid thousands of dollars for this in-depth analysis of our lives? Oh, and that we would have to do this application every time we adopted? It's not a one-and-done situation. Just in case already having one child caused us to partake in criminal activity or put in a gun-shaped pool. Every time we adopted we would go through the whole proving-ourselves-fit-parents thing. We passed by the skin of our teeth. Just kidding. But our answer on "what kind of parent" we would be never got any clearer, in case you were wondering.

This entire home study process took months to complete. The months leading up to the birth of the baby were spent on the home study process instead shopping and being showered. But honestly, we did very little baby prep ahead of time. We were still nervous that the birth mother would change her mind and walk away. It has happened many times in the history of adoption and it will happen again. We had heard all the same stories you've heard. We did buy the basic things like a car seat, a bassinet, and diapers, but we held our excitement close to our hearts, willing ourselves to not get too excited, lest our (or the birth mother's) plans changed. We didn't have any celebratory gender reveals or co-ed baby showers with the decorate-your-onesies stations. But what we did have was an exhaustive 30-page documented analysis of our lives, which I heard really helps you change diapers at 2am.

14

The Strength of Another Mother

I was nervous-sweating again, clutching the steering wheel tightly, as I sat parked outside of where our birth mother was living. I had just texted her letting her know I had arrived to pick her up for her doctor's appointment, as we had pre-arranged. She had missed her last one and our lawyer suggested that she might be more willing to go if I took her. I thought to myself, *what kind of person misses their prenatal appointment? Don't you want to know that everything is going okay?* So there I sat, judging and waiting. Eventually the dark-haired, barely twenty, beautiful young woman carrying *my* daughter emerged from the building, large sunglasses shading her eyes so I could not read her emotions. I started sweating even more. This would be the first time we'd been alone together. Actually, this would be the second time I'd spent time with her, the first being our awkward first-date of a meeting.

She was quiet, but then again, so was I. How do you even start the conversation with the person who is going to *give* you a child? "Hey, thanks so much for being super uncomfortable for nine months on my behalf?" I defaulted to the stupidly boring surface conversational topics instead of all the actual questions that were burning in my mind: like *how do you really feel about all this?* and *what were you like as a child?* But no, weather and favorite movies and TV shows it was while we wound our way through the congested streets to her doctor's office a few miles away. I snuck sideways glances at her every chance I had, trying to memorize the mother's face of my unborn baby.

We arrived at the doctor's office sandwiched in between a Chinese restaurant and a dry cleaner's in a nondescript strip mall. Our birth mother had given her name to the receptionist while I anxiously waited off to the side as her records were pulled, not sure what to expect at this appointment. Would I be allowed to go back with her to see the ultrasound? Would she even invite me back? The dismissive look that crossed over the receptionist's face drew me from my thoughts about myself as her file was pulled and handed over to the nurse. Only when I was walking back to the exam room with her (yes, she graciously invited me and yes, I was allowed) did I see that "adoption plan" was written in bold letters across the top of her file. As we were shown into the room, I distinctly remember sensing disparaging feelings towards our birth mother-feelings that bordered on flat-out rude. They addressed all their comments towards me and showed no restraint in their disdain for our birth mother or her situation. They were abrupt and disrespectful with their questions towards her. I was at a loss to understand why she was treated so poorly, but now could understand clearly why she had not wanted to come to her previous appointments. My mind was quickly backpedaling on my previous perspective of her and was drastically shifted as I watched these interactions unfold in front of me.

Why were they treating her so discourteously? Was it because they thought she would not and did not want to provide for her child and so she didn't deserve to be pregnant? Or because they thought she was young and stupid and needed adoptive parents to rescue her from her situation? Perhaps they thought she should have "taken care of this situation" earlier on. I did not and do not agree with any of these statements. And I watched her as she graciously handled their dis-courteousness with deference and grace. During the months we were matched with our birth mother, I would come to understood her selflessness, her reaching for something better for her unborn baby than what she had experienced. I saw her swallow her pride over and over again as she was dismissed or treated disrespectfully. I witnessed her self-sacrifice as she clearly longed for a different life, one that would have allowed her to keep her unborn baby girl. I distinctly remember a moment at one of these OBGYN appointments where the doctor turned to me and said, "You are doing such an amazing thing. Thank you." And I wanted to say to him, no *she* is doing such an amazing thing. Thank *her* for choosing this. I'm the one who gets a precious newborn baby, all she gets is a ripped apart body and a broken heart. These doctors appointments were eye opening and life changing for me. Every birth mother in our future would be sacrificing on this level. I might not be able to understand this degree of sacrifice, but I would always be grateful for and cherish their decisions.

The few times I visited our birth mother without Jon, taking her to the prenatal doctor's appointments, I counted it as such a gift, seeing the baby move on the ultrasound, hearing her heartbeat. It was one small grace I had been given. I didn't think I'd ever get to experience hearing the heartbeat of my baby in utero or see the grainy ultrasound images. When you make the decision to adopt, you let certain things go. These are a few of the things I had surrendered in our decision to adopt instead of pursue fertility treatments and yet here I was, by the generosity and vulnerability of our birth mother, experiencing them.

Her graciousness in these circumstances made these surreal doctor's appointments bearable. I had accompanied friends to their doctors appointments sitting in the pleasant waiting room, excited and happy with all the staff saying things like "congratulations, you must be so excited." This was an entirely different experience.

There were a few other things I had to let go of as well. In getting to know our birth mothers, I saw what they ate and how they took care of their bodies. I was coming from the world of all-organic everything-don't drink or smoke, exercise daily, take all the vitamins possible in pregnant land. Every pregnant person I had known had the luxury of access to amazing prenatal care, fresh produce, circles of support, and safe living conditions. This was not the case with some of our birth mothers. At first I was horrified and scared that my precious babies they were carrying would suffer the consequences of their actions or situation. Those daily liters of diet coke would have an impact. I'm not saying they wouldn't or didn't, but I am saying that God's hand was on all of our babies. He was protecting their innocent lives and he would take care of the babies *and us* after each was born. I had to let go of the "perfect" pregnancy and let go of trying to control it. Did I once purchase prenatal vitamins and try to convince a birth mother to take them? I did, but I wasn't about to force them down her throat.

Getting to know our first birth mother and understand her world changed my perspective so much. I was in awe that she had actually managed, against great odds, to make an adoption plan and stick to it. That was not what she was surrounded by. Her friends took other routes. There had been lots of pressure for her to do so as well. She walked a lonely road for us. She put up with rude office staff for us. She opened her heart up to heartbreak so that we could have a child. I'm not here to discuss your personal views on abortion or birth control, I'm here to share stories of how four women chose to take an unwanted circumstance and turn it into a massive blessing for us. It is a steep sacrifice that most are not willing to make. So we developed a relationship with this birth mother. We would text in between visits. I'd keep up on how she was doing and she'd ask me how I was feeling and preparing.

These doctor's visits were not the only instances we'd get to spend with this birth mother. But this would be the only time out of all four adoptions that we would actually spend time alone with a birth mother. In the other circumstances we were matched so quickly and the baby born only a few weeks later that we didn't have the time to get to know the other birth mothers. But through a set of unusual circumstances, we would make the drive to Los Angeles and take her to her doctor's appointments or help her with her living situation. We would then spend a couple hours shopping and getting her things she needed or wanted. It was a gift, this time we had together. I was able to see what a lovely, sweet, and kind woman she was.

Of course I was super nervous to build this relationship. At first I wanted to keep an arm's distance and have things remain transactional. It felt like I was going against common sense initiating a relationship. There was an unfounded fear that if I connected with her and got to know her then she'd want to keep her baby. But that is not what God had in mind and that still small voice kept prompting me to ask her the hard questions, be bold in my conversations, and get to know this sweet woman. He wanted to reveal to me the hard and lonely path that a woman faces when she's made an adoption plan. He wanted me to realize what a selfless act was going to bless our lives. Later I would see just how important this connection was.

15

My Darkest Self

About a month before the baby was supposed to be born, a set of events transpired that drove us apart. Do you remember how this birth mother had come to us through our lawyer's colleague? How we ended up paying a second match fee to that company? That was back in late January and in early April it appeared as though some dishonest mismanagement of funds had taken place. We had been sending the adoption facilitator in Los Angeles the monthly living expenses for our birth mother. And if you recall, it was quite a bit more than we had originally anticipated-more than our personal monthly budget. On one of the trips to visit our birth mother, I asked her about her finances and found out that she hadn't been receiving all that we had been sending. Most agencies and lawyers do not want you to discuss the finances of adoption with the birth parents because this could be construed as "buying a baby." The finances are a shaky gray area that varies from agency to agency or lawyer to lawyer and there is not a set standard for how they are handled. Most states require that whoever is responsible for taking care of the birth mother while she's matched with an adoptive couple will handle her living expenses and dole out sums of money each month to the birth mother to cover all the things. The gray area is all the administrative and processing fees that can vary greatly from organization to organization.

To this day, I do not have an accurate accounting of what happened to all our money we sent. But I was MAD to say the least. Here we were scraping the funds together with the consolation that our birth mother's life was being made a bit more comfortable and easier. But that was not the case. Of course we demanded to see all accounting, but this is a very unregulated system and the line item of "operating expenses" and "birth mother expenses" on the spreadsheet sent to us were very vague. Our lawyer couldn't step in due to the contracts in place. This birth mother was technically her colleagues' contact. We were so upset and I shared this all honestly with our birth mother, but our hands were tied. If we wanted this baby, we'd have to stick it out with this dishonest colleague. And we didn't want to jeopardize anything by rocking the boat.

About the same time we were reeling from the deception we were experiencing with the facilitator, our birth mother had to make an emergency visit to the ER. We thought the baby was going to be due mid-April so we thought (as did she) that perhaps she was going into early labor. We hastily packed up the car seat, all our belongings and headed her direction, calling all our friends and family, posting to social media, telling them this was it, ecstatic and nervous that we were going to be parents. By the time we had arrived at the hospital, three hours later, it was clear she wasn't going into labor, but had been dehydrated causing some pre-labor pains. They did another ultrasound to check on the baby and it came back that she was not due for another four weeks-until mid-May. We were all surprised, to say the least. Now this is the part of the story where I show you how abhorrently I acted.

Because we were already on edge with the dishonest behavior of the adoption facilitator, we (I) jumped to conclusions and assumed our birth mother had deceived us. You can probably see how ridiculous this was for us (me) to assume this, but my emotions were so frayed and we already felt like fish out of water in this entire experience. We had no concept of what was normal or if wrong due dates happened often. The professionals we were working with offered us no insights or consolations. Our lawyer could only speak from her experiences, but she didn't know our birth mother personally. We didn't know what to believe or whom to trust. We were also reeling from the idea of needing to find ten more weeks of living expenses for her. Like I mentioned, it was already doubling our budget each month, so two, almost three more months seemed like it would be impossible. This is how close we were to being completely drained financially. So, we helped our birth mother get settled back at home after her hospital visit and then made the long drive home spiraling in all our thoughts.

By the time we arrived back at our house, we had decided that we needed to let our birth mother go and sever all ties with our lawyer's colleague, our birth mother's facilitator. We would lose so much money in doing this, as we wouldn't be refunded any expenses because it was our decision to back out, but we felt like we were in the middle of a dishonest situation and we didn't know how to move forward. In the contracts we had signed, we had agreed that if we canceled the match for any reason, we would lose all the money we had already paid. We weren't sure if our birth mother was using us for our money and then was going to keep the baby after all (yes, this does happen). We weren't sure how much "extra" expenses the adoption facilitator would ask us for and we didn't have anything extra left. We told our lawyer we wanted out. We told our birth mother we couldn't keep on with her adoption facilitator, and if she decided she still wanted to place the baby with us, then she should call our lawyer when she was in labor. We didn't want to be involved anymore. See? I told you it was disgraceful. I still am ashamed of the way I acted towards this sweet woman. But we couldn't see beyond our disappointment. I responded in fear and self-preservation. We acted selfishly, thinking not about our birth mother and all she was experiencing but only about how we were feeling in this circumstance.

We had driven down to Los Angeles thinking we were going to come home with a precious newborn baby and instead we walked away from it all. We were crushed. Shattered. We fielded hundreds of "What happened?" from everyone we knew and telling the story over and over again didn't get any less painful. They hadn't been on the same emotional journey we had, they didn't know our birth mother, so they supported us and backed our decision. Everyone was convinced we had been scammed. We had been so publicly supported in this adoption by not only family and friends, but Jon's co-workers, my wedding industry friends, and the community we lived in. We had to tell everyone we knew and all I wanted to do was curl up in bed and cry.

"This is how I feel today. Shattered. I've lost all my petals. Many of you know we've been planning to adopt and thought the due date was this week. Through a series of unforeseen and unpredictable circumstances (and a lot of withheld information) we found out that the due date is actually 5 weeks from now and most likely we will not be adopting the little baby girl. We feel like the rug has been pulled out from underneath us, but this is when we get to trust and believe that God is bigger than all this and has a perfect plan for us. We want to thank all of you, friends and strangers alike, for your support and encouragement these last few crazy months." (Posted on social media with an image of a shattered flower, petals strew across our dining room table.)

Did I feel like having faith at that moment? Did I really feel like trusting that God had a perfect plan for us? No, I most certainly did not. But this was one of those moments were the years of practicing relinquishing came back in full force. I had lost my heart before. I had had all my plans striped away before. This was not the first time I felt the rug pulled out from underneath me and my petals shattered. The difference between then and now was that I was ready to willingly have faith, even when I didn't feel like it. Sometimes it is in the darkest moments, when your heart is losing focus and black is creeping into the corners of your vision, that you understand with the utmost conviction that God's plan is bigger than what you can see. It just must be. Even if you don't feel like it, you know it with conviction.

This is how Jon and I felt when we walked away from our birth mother. Yes, for sure we were reeling from what we were doing, but we also knew we were doing the right thing. My heart was still broken, however, and I could barely manage life through all my tears. I called my sister to come pack away the precious few baby things we had prepared because I couldn't face it. We had been sustained throughout this whole process by the anticipation of welcoming a new baby, now all that had crashed down around us and we felt drained, empty, and most definitely broke.

We decided we just needed a few weeks to gather ourselves and then we'd allow our lawyer to present our portfolio to any birth mothers she had. We had almost completed all the exhaustive steps for adoption, we couldn't just throw away all that time and money. With adoption lawyers and agencies, if the birth mother (or in this case, the adoptive parents) decides to walk away from an adoption plan and keep the baby, the adoptive parents lose the money they spent towards the birth mother expenses. However the agency or lawyer will use the funds paid for the match fee to find another match for the adoptive parents. That is exactly what our lawyer planned to do for us. However, since we did not want to work with her colleague anymore, we forfeited any money we had paid to her. For us that was huge, but if our lawyer had another birth mother that had low (I mean, super low) living expenses then maybe we could do it. So we tucked all our hopes about the future away for a few weeks, pulled our hearts together, and relished in the unexpected calm and quiet.

Well, relatively calm and quiet.

I had spent years building up my floral design company to handle multiple weddings on a weekend. I had built a team that could operate without me and I had staffed all my upcoming weddings as though I was going to be home with a new baby, but instead I threw myself into them and enjoyed the distraction. Since January we had been so focused on completing all the steps for adoption and caring for our birth mother that we hadn't realized how stressful and distracting it had all been. When we let it all go, we released the tension we had been holding for four months. We were able to turn our attention back to our normal routine and enjoy our peaceful, full life.

16

An Undeserved Gift

I t had been almost exactly one month since we had walked away
from our adoption plans, and finally the sting of heartbreak had
worn away. We had embraced the busy wedding season to fill our
heads with anything but thoughts of the baby we weren't adopting. I
had thrown myself back into work with renewed vigor (some might
call it deflection, I call it self-preservation). And I had just finished
a weekend with two massive weddings back to back which had left
my mind like mushy peas and my body like a pile of limp spaghetti.
I had treated myself to a post -wedding glass of wine and a massage
after all the hard aching work of the weekend. Freshly showered, book
in hand, and sitting on my bed's edge ready to tuck in for the night,
my phone rang. It was our birth mother. *Our birth mother.* My mind
started instantly spinning.

She said she felt like she was getting close to labor and still really wanted
us to be the adoptive parents. She had not found anyone else she liked
(I guess her facilitator had presented her with other options). She had
felt connected to us the first time she had met us and she knew we
were the right parents for her baby girl. Can we just talk about how

brave she was? We had basically shut her down and written her off and yet she came back with conviction. She knew in her heart what she wanted and she was determined to see it through. She told us that she had walked away from her facilitator and was not working with her anymore. She had called our lawyer herself and wanted to work with us.

We were thrilled, but also so, so nervous. What if we dove back into this only to have it pulled out from underneath us again? Looking back, I realize how foolish this all sounds. What person, after being so heartily rejected, would insist that this was what they wanted? She was convinced that what we had shared, leading up to the point where we walked away, was the life she wanted for her unborn child. We unwittingly made her jump through hoops to prove herself when really, it should have been us proving we were worthy to be chosen by her. At this point our birth mother didn't need anything else from us, she just needed us. We took a big breath and committed to her again. We trusted her. After all, hadn't she just proved herself to us? Seeking us out against all odds, putting herself in uncomfortable situations to cancel her contract with our lawyer's colleague, calling our lawyer (whom she'd never met), and pursuing us? I'm humbled to think that she was brave enough to do what she thought was right, when it was definitely not easy. Weren't we supposed to be the ones saving her? And instead, she was saving us from ourselves, from our own fears. She was brave and strong-so much more so than us. We packed up a few baby things for the hospital, installed the car seat, and told no one outside of our immediate family. Then on Monday night, a few days later, I was once again settling down to read a book in bed (not sure I ever finished that book), and she called. She was in labor, headed to the hospital, and wanted us to come. *Yes she was sure.*

Let's just pause a moment and all take a deep breath together. One month prior we had walked away from everything, trusting God had a better plan for us. And now here we were, right back with the same birth mother. What had we gained from all that mess? Why had we needed to go through that heartbreak and trouble? We needed to learn humility. *I* needed to learn humility. I'm pretty sure Jon is already loads humble enough. We needed to see that this was, without a shadow of a doubt, the baby meant for us. I wonder if we had gone through with the adoption as planned, without walking away, without having our birth mother seek us out again, if we would have questioned the rightness of the situation. Would we have always questioned if this baby was for us? But now all doubts were driven from our mind as we fully embraced the plan before us. God had provided *and* taken our hearts on a journey that would be crucial in future adoptions. Of course at the time we had no idea there would be three more adoptions, but we would walk into each one a million times more confident of God's hands holding everything.

So we drove with the excited nervousness that any expectant parents do (but without anyone writhing in pain in our car). We had no idea what to expect when we arrived at the hospital. We didn't even know how to check in. We hadn't been prepped with a plan or what we were even supposed to do. Our birth mother had been walked through a birthing plan by her adoption service provider (a neutral third party provided by the state to make sure the birth mother is aware of what they are doing prior to birth and not being coerced into anything), and had actually requested we be present with her in the room. That's all we knew. For all the exhaustive research of our personal lives to make sure we were fit to be parents, no one actually instructed us on how to be new parents in adoption. We didn't take any birthing classes, get a tour of the hospital, or receive instructions on how things would go down. We didn't even know where the labor and delivery wing was. When we arrived at the hospital we were asked by security what our relationship to the patient was and we had to wait while they phoned the nurse's station, digging up the records to see if we truly were allowed in. This was the beginning of one of the four uncomfortable hospital experiences we had. We were surprised to learn that being adoptive parents in the labor and delivery wing, and then later in the maternity ward, was a little like being the large elephant in the room. No one really addresses you directly. You're kind of just standing around in the way. Every nurse and doctor has their personal beliefs on adoption and they are not shy about expressing those. Fortunately for us, this first hospital experience was mild compared to the others. But it didn't make it less awkward.

We were escorted directly to her delivery room. And there we were: our birth mother, her boyfriend (not the baby's father), Jon, and me. It was uncomfortable to say the least. Even with all the attempted relationship building and the sweetest demeanor of our birth mother, no one can prepare you for the heaviness of the room. There were no squeals of excitement, joyful "you can do this". The air felt delicate, tender, even sorrowful. We felt self-conscious and like we didn't know what to do or where to stand. We felt like we were in the midst of a tragic ballet and our hands felt too big for our bodies, our feet too clumsy beneath us. This woman struggling in labor, just feet away, was going to give us her baby. We were unworthy of this gift. We were acutely aware of the sacrifice she was making and the loss she would feel. We didn't know where to put our bodies. How to stay out of the way and yet be a support to her. By the saving grace of God her labor was short-only a couple of hours. And then it was like the sun broke out from behind the clouds, chasing away the mist that had shrouded the room.

I cannot tell you what an amazing experience it is to watch a baby being born. Let alone watch your own baby being born. There I was in the dead of the night, in a small delivery room on the rough side of LA, holding the legs of the woman who was changing my life forever. She had not only graciously allowed both Jon and I to be present in the delivery room, something that does not happen often in these situations, but also be an active participant in the delivery. Once again, our birth mother set aside her self-consciousness to include us and make us part of the story. A favor we will always cherish. The image of our baby's head crowning and her soft cries filling the room is seared into my mind. The doctor handed me the scissors to cut the umbilical cord and then, a few minutes later, handed me the baby.

Our baby.

17

The Other Side

I could continue on with our story right now, but I want to share something else with you. We had been feeling God go before us and lay the ground work for this adoption. The most amazing part is that this story is not one-sided. I recently asked this birth mother about her experience through all this, and this is what she said:

"To start from the beginning, I remember sitting in the room with my facilitator [our lawyer's colleague], this was after meeting her for the first time, or maybe the first two times, and this is where she gave me a stack of books of potential families. Your little white book was on top. When I started turning the pages I started to cry and it was something like a magnet in my heart. You guys reminded me so much of my god family who had taken me in when I was five, I could tell you were kind, safe and the kind of people I always wanted as parents, or even to be myself. The best way I can describe it is when you are trying on wedding dresses and you feel this big feeling in your chest when you have found "the one", tears and everything. I just felt a tug in my heart that this is where my baby was supposed to go. So we can fast forward to when we started getting the vibe that the facilitator [our lawyer's colleague] was shady. I remember having my own reasons as

to why I felt like she was just *not right*, when she would buy me the same groceries every week and I couldn't shop for them myself. I don't remember exactly your reasons, but I remember we were having the same idea about her. I remember you being the one to break the news to me that you wouldn't be proceeding forward. When it happened, I felt like the carpet got ripped out from underneath me. I felt like I did something wrong. I felt disrespected in a way. I felt a feeling of abandonment or rejection, which I was way too familiar with. I sat there with my feelings at eight months pregnant and I just told myself, no. This isn't going to be like this. There has to be a way, I don't want anybody else with my baby. Reflecting on the books in the beginning, everybody seemed cataloged, or like those cheesy lifetime movies (not the ones that are actually good) and I just didn't want to even interview with others. Like I said when I saw your book and then got to know you even more, that was the life I wanted. That was the family I wanted to create and if the closest I could get to that was making sure my unborn baby was given that, I was going to do it. There was no second option for me, I didn't even want to think about it. I knew in my heart of hearts that this baby was meant for you and you were meant for this baby. I don't remember how we ended up working with your lawyer and I don't remember who broke the news to her colleague. I do remember feeling like we had to ease back into trusting each other again. I know I had betrayed your trust in me a few times back then, and when you walked away, I felt a little concerned about you guys as well. But the "right" feeling I had in my heart was strong enough to get over the concerned part. Because I just knew this is how it is supposed to be. I'm not God, and it could have gone a million different ways and we [could have] never spoke again. But I do think God made it happen from the moment I saw your book, to when we were in the delivery room together and you guys had made it right on time driving through the night."

Okay, can we just talk about amazing? So basically when I was devastated that we walked away from this birth mother, she was upset as well. She had claimed us for her unborn child and would not accept any other option. Her resilience and strength was (and still is) awe-inspiring to me. This is what I want to leave with you; God was working. We only saw the partial picture, and not until writing this book and asking her for her side of things, did I fully see the whole picture.

18

How to Face Your Fears

Our baby.

My vision narrowed to this tiny form in my arms. Her dark hair, her soft skin. She tucked herself against me. I glanced up to our birth mother, still struggling through the last dredges of labor and her tears told me enough. She had requested in her birth plan that the baby-*our baby*-be handed directly to us. It was one more gift she gave us. Those precious first few moments were ours. I cannot even begin to imagine the sacrifice even those moments cost her. It seemed as though the room held still for a few moments as if in awe of what was transpiring. Then a whirlwind of activity took place.

As Jon and I stared down at this precious little life cocooned in stillness, the nurses prepped our birth mother to move. Later we would reflect on this quick movement-this rush to move her out. It was as though everyone was uncomfortable with the situation-everyone except the birth mother and us, the three people who mattered most. It seemed as though the nurses wanted to separate us as soon as possible, whisking us off to separate rooms. In all that rush, we never had a moment to just be with each other and allow our birth mother to see our gratitude, our awe of what she had just done. Instead, it felt like she was being treated as a means to an end, a vessel for us. Not allowed the dignity to remain together because we were not on equal ground. Remember how I mentioned the doctor's office visits? How I was treated like the savior swooping in to save the day? This felt ten times worse.

If I could go back, I would tell myself to put aside the fear that she would change her mind in the moment, be assertive enough to tell the hospital staff to stop their activity, and allow myself to really truly show our birth mother how much she had just blessed us. I would be brave enough to look her in the eye and give her the words that were swirling in my head and heart. I would show the hospital staff the respect I had for her and not allow their discomfort with the situation to dominate. Over the next three births, I would become more bold, but unfortunately the situations would not improve much and the uncomfortable feelings radiating throughout the room would only get worse. I would advocate for a moment without the rushing of the hospital staff. I would ask for a quiet moment alone with her. I would allow the words that hung heavy in the room to be spoken. I would actually say the words that scared me to death for fear that acknowledging the action out loud would break the magical spell of adoption: "Thank you for this gift. For this child. We will forever be grateful to you."

To allow yourself to be known and to have your desires be known is scary. To express those desires when at the mercy of someone else is downright terrifying. The truth is, the birth mother is allowed to change her mind about the adoption. She can change her mind within the first 30 days after the birth. Unless, while in the hospital or shortly thereafter, she signs a paper relinquishing that right. Even then, she can change her mind within 24 hours after that paper is signed. After those time frames have expired, she can no longer go back on her adoption plan and take back the baby.

With another one of our babies this did happen. The birth mother did not sign the paperwork relinquishing her rights, giving us the assurance we so desperately wanted. We even left the hospital, went home, and she still hadn't signed. Two weeks went by and she *still* hadn't signed. One day I looked down at our precious tiny newborn and I realized I wasn't calling her by the name she had been given by us. I could tell I was withholding, not attaching and I knew exactly why. I also realized I couldn't do this to a precious new baby, I needed to attach. Give her everything I had. So I faced my deepest and scariest fear and messaged the birth mother and I boldly asked her why she hadn't signed the paper and was she going to change her mind and request we bring the baby back to her?

Our lawyer was floored I'd be this bold. But let's be honest, I would have much rather known then wait out another two weeks wondering if the birth mother was going to change her mind. I would also, as hard as it might be, want to re-unite our precious new gift with the birth mother if that's the direction this all went, if that's the plan God had in mind. That baby needed to bond with their parent immediately and I wasn't going to let my fears stand in the way of this. Do you know what the birth mother said? She said she hadn't signed because it felt too aggressive. Even though she knew she had to let go and place the baby with us, it just seemed too painful. She'd rather let the month slip by as she mourned her loss and let her baby slip out of her hands. So heartbreaking. I think her raw emotions would have petrified me if this had been our first adoption, but after our other experiences I knew that this grief was normal and to be expected. And her willingness to even place her baby with us, when she so longed to keep her, was proof enough that she would not be asking for the baby back. She had already faced the hardest decision, placing that baby in our arms and letting us walk out the door.

After all we had done to prepare for this adoption, and after all the conversations our birth mother had with the lawyers, agencies, and adoption service provider, she STILL could have changed her mind, leaving us at the mercy of her will. Not only that, she could have changed her mind in the height of the hormonal onslaught that comes after birth. In my opinion, this law does not benefit anyone and here's why: if the adoption agency, lawyer, or facilitator has done their job well, the birth mother will have already been walked through the repercussions of their actions. She will have been warned about the reality of what she is about to do, counseled through her post-birth hormones. She will have been told what to expect and how she might feel. She will have been given the opportunity multiple times before the birth to change her mind. She will have been given every possible out until she is 100% sure an adoption plan is what she wants for her unborn child.

But, in my observation, this is not how it usually goes. It seems as though agencies, lawyers and facilitators are too nervous to talk openly about all this for fear of losing their client. For fear that their birth mother will walk away. But this is the time when the birth mother should change her mind-when she can seek out pregnancy resources and make a plan for raising a child. Not in the hospital with no plan, no support system, and even no car seat to get the baby home. Or worse, 30 days later after everyone has settled into new rhythms.

These thoughts lurked in the back of my mind as I held our newborn baby, unable to express all that I was feeling. Our first birth mother was ushered in one direction while we were escorted in other, my hand tightly gripped on the plastic baby bassinet. Our eyes met only briefly through all the hospital staff and chaotic movements around us. My heart was breaking for this sweet young lady who was saying goodbye to the baby she had carried in her womb for the last 40 weeks. The woman who had pursued her plan for the little life growing inside of her against all opposition-objecting to the suggested abortions, putting up with being shamed, and choosing us even after we had walked away-protecting the precious baby at all costs. Now she was opening her hands and letting her go. A sacrifice so deep I struggle to fully comprehend it. My heart was torn in two as I ecstatically held my newborn's tiny fingers in mine. And that is what adoption is, your hands so full they overflow holding pain and sorrow tangled with immense joy and thankfulness.

19

Tacos and Tequila

W e were escorted out of the labor and delivery room to the maternity wing without so much as a goodbye to our birth mother. That wasn't intentional, we just didn't know what was going on, after all, this was our first birth experience. Remember the big elephants in the room? That was us. The baby was the hospital's patient, not us. We were guests of the baby, only allowed to stay because, well honestly, the nursing staff would otherwise have to keep an eye on the baby as there was no general nursery room. Additionally, we were told if the wing became too crowded we (not the baby), would be kicked out of our room to make space for actual patients. So as long as the hospital wasn't too busy, we were allowed to stay in a room. I think insurance has a lot to do with this as the baby is on the mother's (often medicaid) insurance. We spent the better part of the next 24 hours feeling forgotten. Unlike your typical mother and baby situation (where both the mother and the baby are patients and are celebrated), we were riding on the goodness of the hospital.

So off we went to the maternity wing and proceeded to spend the next day and night as unwanted party guests. Learning how to change, feed, and care for this new baby with no instructions or nursing staff checking in on us, only the baby. It was actually rather surreal. Since we had not been parents in a maternity ward before, we did not know what to expect. Medical decisions for the baby were made without our consent. Hospital formula was fed to her instead of the formula I had so carefully researched. She was swaddled up in hospital blankets and hospital clothes instead of being allowed in the soft lovely blankets I had brought. Very little deference was turned our way. It was as though she wasn't even our baby. Honestly, I don't think the hospital thought of her as ours.

Again, we were just bystanders in the room, and of course we were on our own. Since we were not the actual patient, we weren't responsible for any of the hospital costs. But that also meant we didn't receive any meals, advice on how to care for this tiny newborn who was new to us, or even told where the ladies locker room was for a shower. Not to mention, Jon was technically only allowed to remain in the room if I was there. Upon the delivery of our baby, security bracelets were assigned-one to the birth mother, one to the baby, and one to me. No, there was not a fourth for Jon, my husband, the father of our baby. The hospital "doesn't do that." So for the 24 hours we remained in the hospital, anytime I needed to leave the room, I'd have to call a nurse to take the baby. Adoption is just not accommodated in the hospital setting. However, it did result in some funny stories, great Mexican food, and the sneaking of celebratory cocktails into our room since no one was checking on us.

If you had told my twenty-something self who had so desperately longed for children, that this was to be my story, I would have fiercely protested. Surely that was not what my gracious and loving God had intended for me. I would have had a birth experience that was warm, celebratory, and full of laughter. But see, this was the journey I had to take for all those years leading up to our first adoption. I spent years, *years*, practicing letting go of my expectations. And when I say practicing, I mean that it had been forced practice time. Like the hell week leading up to the big match. Learning to let go of the significant loves of my life and leaning into whatever God had planned for me instead, taught me resilience. Living single while others had moved on to different phases of life had taught me thankfulness. Prioritizing family and a community that loves me had taught me to value what was important. My hands had been forced to let go of my expectations and dreams so many times in the previous 15 years, that by the time we endured this unorthodox birth experience, we embraced it and laughed our way through. We did not wallow in the loss of normalcy. We did not bemoan our poor fate. Rather we observed it like bystanders of a comical play and, like I said, we snuck in margaritas and tacos and celebrated our new precious little life in a forgotten hospital room in the middle of Los Angeles.

Meanwhile, our birth mother was moved to her own room while we were getting settled with the baby in ours. I'm not exactly sure what transpired in her room, but around 12 hours after the baby had been born we were told she wanted to see us to say goodbye because she was leaving against medical orders. She would rather recover at home. Honestly, I don't blame her. The way the hospital staff had dismissed her and treated her as less than human would be uncomfortable to say the least. Then lying in a bed in the same building as your newborn baby and not being able to mother would be devastating. I'm not surprised she wanted to leave. She hadn't been made to feel wanted or valuable. So we took ourselves and the baby over to her room to say goodbye. We all teared up, all knew the weight of what was happening and the blessing she had given us. We were able to hug her and thank her properly for what she had given us. Then she was gone. That was the last time we would see her.

A surreal 24 hours, one movie about breastfeeding (totally applicable), and some signed paperwork later, we were released from our forgotten room of the hospital. We packed up our sweet precious baby and started that very cautious drive home that every new parent takes. We looked at each other as we were pulling out and said, "They're just going to let us leave? Walk out with this baby?" In all our adoptions, the surrealness of this moment would always hit hard. The reality of walking into the hospital one day and walking out the next with someone else's baby with no physical repercussions, no birthing classes, no prep whatsoever, would always catch us off guard. And since there always remained the possibility in every adoption that the birth mother could change her mind, our emotions were constantly all over the place. Until that final relinquishment paperwork was signed, the swinging pendulum of emotions takes a very grounded faith to weather. I spent the car drive home ordering things off our just-in-case-we-actually-bring-the-baby-home Amazon list and posting to social media ,"Surprise! We have a baby!"

Our very little prep also included telling very few people prior to our baby's birth. When the adoption had seemingly fallen apart back in April, we had struggled to wade through the emotions of announcing the disaster and the condolences that followed afterwards. Well-meaning individuals would ask prying questions that would dredge up all the emotions we were processing. I don't mean to sound ungrateful for the way people cared for us, it just felt painful and embarrassing. As though we should have known better. As if adoption often ends in heartbreak-and didn't you know? (We heard that more than once.) Our hearts were tender. So when our birth mother called us when in labor, we decided to only tell our family. We would wait until we were sure we were coming home with a baby before announcing it to the world again. So on our drive home, I simply posted we were on our way home and introduced the world to our new baby girl. It was simple and yet huge. Of course any new baby's birth is huge. Anytime you add a baby into the mix it's huge. But what I was most struck by was-how did this just happen? How did we, with only a couple months of effort, end up with this perfect sweet baby girl? How did we deserve this? And this how I came to truly understand God's grace.

This sweet baby felt like exactly what she was, an unwarranted magnificent gift. It was not lost on either of us how undeserving we were of this gift. We did not bring this child into the world and yet we had been entrusted with her care. She is not ours, yet here were are raising her. Hold up, you might be thinking "but she is *yours*." You adopted her, that's exactly what that means. And yes, legally, she did belong to us (well, not quite yet, but we'll get there.) We are responsible for her well-being, her medical decisions, the feeding and caring of her. But she was also placed in our arms as chosen stewards of her future. Her birth mother made the decision to allow us to raise her instead of raising her herself, with no strings attached. But we were also aware enough to know that our future daughter, full of questions, would want to know about her birth mother. Our daughter would want to understand why her birth mother chose us. She would most likely want to know her, meet her, and possibly have a relationship with her.

In all our adoptions, only a small portion of the paperwork addressed the issue of whether we wanted a closed or open adoption and what the birth mother's preferences were as well. We had selected "open" in each of our adoptions. Initially this made us-and everyone we spoke to-nervous. What did this mean exactly? Were we going to have regular visits with the birth mother? Would we be in constant communication letting them infiltrate every parenting decision of our lives? Were we going to have to become friends with the birth mothers?

I can confidently say, after four different birth mothers, all selecting "open", it means exactly the opposite of what is going through your head right now. It means that we have the possibility and the potential to be in contact should we want to. Whether that was immediately after the birth or sometime in the future. It also means that the birth mother could have contact with us should she want to. Wait, hold up. That's the scary part, right? Yes and no. Let's think through this. A birth mother makes an adoption plan because she cannot care for the child herself. If she was interested in making parenting decisions and shouldering the responsibility of raising a child, there are plenty of resources available to her for raising her own child. An adoption plan is made because raising the child is not an option. Whatever her reasoning is, she is making a plan better than the options before her. She is (usually) aware of the weight of this. How easy do you think it is to carry a child for 280 days, birth the baby through hard pain, and then pass it off to someone else? It's not easy. Not at all. So this birth mother has likely faced this truth and still made the decision to place her baby for adoption. She is not looking to step in on your parenting decisions and weigh in on raising a child. I can't speak for everyone, but four out of four birth mothers have proven me right, so I'd say the odds are pretty good.

20

What Open Means

I was exhausted, the bags deep under my eyes. I had never done well without sleep, but this newborn-not-sleeping schedule was beyond. It was so much harder than I had anticipated. I had just settled her down for the night, all of her four-day-old self swaddled in tight and tucked into her little bed, my fingers crossed she'd sleep until midnight before screaming us awake again. My nerves were frayed, my brain not processing properly. And then she texted. Our birth mother texted.

It was an innocent enough of "How are you doing, how is the baby?" type of thing. But my mind started to whirl and spin. I replied with the normal "good and tired" newborn line and then asked after her. She was tired, her body hurt, she missed us and the baby (I'm thinking the baby mostly). My palms started to sweat and my emotions started to climb. Was this how it was going to be? Was I going to have to balance the sweetness and challenges of our new precious baby and the postpartum emotions of our birth mother? I could barely hold my own emotions in check, let alone carry those of a newborn and a mourning mother. I started to panic. Had we made the wrong choice consenting to an open adoption? Would she miss the baby so much that she'd hop in the car and come find us? Would she want us to come down and hang out with her? My 10 PM sleep-deprived brain was not doing me any favors and it continued to add fueling thoughts to my hysterical brain.

A couple of messages later she said good night, and I went back to my spiraling thoughts when I should have been sleeping in the precious few hours before I would need to be up feeding the baby again. Let's just say it was a rough night as I shuffled through all the different scenarios and *did not at all* take any of my thoughts captive. The next morning I texted our lawyer, my anxiety at an all-time high. I so desperately wanted to have the "normal" family life that I had longed for. Sure we had gotten here a different way than all our friends, but now that we had the baby, it should all plod along normally, right? These messages from our birth-mother had thrown that theory out the window as I panicked myself into a corner. Our lawyer quickly assured us that this was considered expected behavior from a birth mother-especially one that we had befriended-but that in her experience it would taper off. After a bit, the birth mothers usually lost the desire to be in communication for whatever reason.

Having our lawyer's voice of reason calm my inner turmoil made me stop to think about the deep sorrow that surrounded these words. Yes, the birth mother had chosen this path. But my freak out response was also considered typical (according to our lawyer) and *that* made me sad. In what world are we living where when someone gives you their child born from their body, we fear them, and feel the loss of said child? Of course they will mourn - that is mentally and physically healthy. Why do we not make room for this mourning and give it the space and time it needs *without* panicking in fear like I did?

107

What was driving my panicking thoughts was that our birth mother would miss her baby so much that she would want to take her back. But she had already signed the relinquishing paperwork and it wouldn't be possible at this point. Additionally, the fears that she would want to come alongside us and be a part of our lives and that would be a *bad* thing, took hold of my heart. I wanted to be in charge of who and what was in my sweet precious newborn's life. And I deemed her birth mother to be a threat to our sheltered little nucleus. Why, you might wonder? Because she'd be a bad influence on our child? Because she would influence her to make decisions we didn't approve of like that crazy aunt everyone has and tries to avoid at holidays? Because we feared the birth mother would try to be too involved in our lives making them messy? Because what if our baby decided she loved her birth mother more than me?

Ah, there it is. The root of all my fear.

The fear that my adopted child would choose someone to love other than me. Well, isn't that interesting? My mind immediately protected its territory: this was my child now, who and what was in her life would be our decision, right? No, wrong. (I bet you saw that coming, didn't you?).

Remember all those lessons in relinquishment I learned over the past years leading up to this adoption? All those moments that felt outside of my control had led me time and time again to listen to the still small voice in my soul that was nudging me to open my hands and let go. ((the need "to be in charge" issue just keeps resurfacing.) *Let go of control.* Relinquishing what I was clinging tightly to in favor of what God had yet to reveal. So when I stopped my racing heart, pacified by the wise counsel of our lawyer, I could hear that still small voice in my heart once again. What if what our birth mother needed was the reassurance that she had made the right decision? What if she needed to hear that this was a good and solid decision even though her body and her mind were hurting. My soul told me that she needed to feel heard and loved. Just in this moment she was broken and needing loving. She had no agenda for the baby or the future. And so that's what I tried to do in my tired, exhausted state. Listen and encourage her. Honestly, looking back now I have no idea how I did. But I will tell you this: is she still in contact with us? Yes, absolutely. Have I had the opportunity to reach out to her and ask her important questions as my (her) daughter grows? Yes. Was I able to ask her to write her side of the story you read previously? Yes. I strongly believe that had I let my fear push her away, we would have none of these. My life is richer because she remains in it.

So, that leaves us with the looming question of, what then, does an open adoption look like? For us it has meant that after the birth of every child, we'd hear from the birth mother for a couple weeks. Texts here and there asking how everyone was doing. It also meant that, for a few of our babies, the birth mothers asked for pictures of the baby, often specifically with their siblings in the family setting. In our adoption agreements with the birth mothers, each requested a similar amount of contact. Pictures every six months and occasional (not in person) contact for checking in. However, and this is a big however, desires change over the years and we have found that while each of our birth mothers, save one, asked for these updates and pictures every six months their contact has dwindled as the child has grown.

I think this is natural, but it also makes me sad. It's not for lack of loving the baby they placed with us, but for the simple fact that life moves on. At first, we were scared we'd have to keep up with a series of updates for the entirety of our children's lives, but we have come to realize an open adoption means *possibility*. The possibility they can reach out to us and also the possibility that we can reach out to them. Recently, I asked one birth mother which holidays were important to her in her childhood, what her family was like, and what interests she had as a child. Her answers are helping me form a cultural identity for our Asian American daughter. Without this open adoption connection, this would not be possible.

I have one more not-so-small thought about this. If you recall from earlier, Jon had placed a baby for adoption in his early college years. It was common at the time to agree to a closed adoption. Let the adoptive family take the child and raise it and let the birth parents move on. Unfortunately, this closed adoption choice has weighed heavily on Jon. I cannot speak for his biological son, but when his son's 18th birthday came around, Jon was hoping he'd reach out to him for contact. That's when his biological son would have access to the adoption records and, as a legal adult, would be able to contact Jon if he wished. Unfortunately for Jon, it was a one-way street. The only way for Jon to contact the adoptive parents and his biological son was through the lawyer with whom they had finalized the adoption. So soon after his biological son's 18th birthday, Jon reached out to the adoption lawyer they had used and updated his contact information, asking it be passed along to the adoptive parents. He hoped, excited even, about being in contact with his biological son. We had adopted two children and had a deeper understanding of the whole process by then. He was hopeful he could build a bridge with his biological son and be there for him, should he have any questions about Jon's family or history. There wasn't any preconceived ideas that Jon would become like a father figure, usurping the role of his adoptive father. But he was hopeful that his biological son would want to know him. So he relied on that one lawyer to pass along his contact information. There was nothing else he could do. So he waited. For five years he waited.

I think after all we had been through with adopting our own children, Jon's compassion for each birth mother (and the birth father, if present) grew in those five years. Nothing will ever replace the role of adoptive parents and the love and care they show their children. But the biological connection between a child and parent is real, and we would be remiss to ignore it. We would be flat out stupid to think our children wouldn't at the very least be curious about their genetics or biological family history. And eventually they'll hit 18 and do what they want anyway, so why not be on their team, right? Help them navigate the complex emotions they might experience when searching and discovering their genetic history? Jon's personal experiences helped shape the way we perceive the future of our children. We were (and are) fully aware that we would need to raise our children with our hands and hearts open to the unknowns ahead. This is putting into practice the relinquishment we have practiced for years leading up to these adoptions. These children have been given to us and, for as long as they are with us, we will love and care for them the best we are able. But in the end we cannot hold tightly to who they are or who they will become. If this sounds scary to you, it is. It feels scary too. It feels outside of our control and honestly, it *is* outside of our control. But ultimately we live more fully when we try not to control our lives. We live better, breath deeper, and our hearts are at peace when we hold our hands open. We know firsthand from previous experiences how God has gone before us, creating a path, opening doors, giving us the tools we needed at the time we needed them. We have had an opportunity with each child to trust that God has always had and will always continue to have a hand over their little lives.

21

To Tell or Not To Tell

We're gathered around the dining table with half-full plates scattered in front of us, as the voices of multiple conversations spill over each other, as usual. Sure, I'd love to teach them all not to interrupt and to wait their turn to speak, but have you ever sat at a table over dinner with four siblings? It is absolute chaos as little voices ask for the rice to be passed, or request that their chicken be cut, let alone the excitement of telling about the afternoon of walking down in the creek bed and finding super large yet-to-be identified bones of an animal. It is a happy chaos you can't quell. But as I looked around the table taking it all in, there was one little face who was not joining in the laughing, she wasn't asking for things to be passed or food to be cut. She was sitting looking down at her plate. Jon seemed to notice the same minute I did and asked what might be bothering her Big tears filled her eyes as she replied that she missed her birth mother and wanted to see her.

Did you start to panic on my behalf as you read that? You had followed along happily with our rambunctious dinner until I reached that point? Friends have witnessed these teary-eyed confessions from our children, and the endless stream of questions about their birth parents that come out of nowhere. And usually right on the heels of these outburst we are asked by them, "When did you decide to tell them they were adopted?"

The reality is, it has simply always been part of our conversation with them and around them. We would speak openly about our adoptions (with discretion, of course), in front of them. When we were ready to adopt our second, we told our first born our plans. She was young enough to understand a brother was coming, but not old enough to understand where he would come from. Then by the third adoption, our two older ones understood we go to the hospital to pick up our babies. This mama doesn't carry them in her tummy. We have naturally worked their birth stories into our conversations that come up about where they come from, how babies are born, and why I do not carry children in my own womb. We do not shy away from questions they ask about their birth mothers or fathers. Interestingly, one of our daughters is the spitting image of me when I was young and one son looks just like Jon did as a baby, as is often pointed out when we meet new people. It always leads one of the children to ask what their birth parents looked like. No matter how many times we've already described them, they seem to always want to hear it again.

We love that our personalities and characteristics are infused into them, but we are also quick to point out the characteristics they have received genetically, the best we can recall. Your hair is just as dark and luxurious as we remember your mother's being. You have her eyes. That quick smile and endless stream of conversations definitely came from your birth father. We want them to understand and feel like they should never shy away from where they came from and it is a wonderful blessing to have each other even though we are all different.

The bottom line is: We have always talked about it. We talk about it now. And we will keep talking about it. While the conversations may be hard at times for my tender heart, I do not ever want to shy away from the truth of who they are. I never want them to feel embarrassed to ask, or feel as though the subject of their birth parents is taboo. What precious little information we have on each birth parent we try to share with each of them. Do you recall all the paperwork that we had received on each birth parent after we agreed to the match? This is why we jealously hoarded any information we were given. We knew we would want to pass it along as gifts to each child. The more details we had about them, their likes, their dislikes, their family history, their heritage, this was (and is) the most precious gold we can give each child.

Though admittedly, this is sometimes painful for us. Every time a child asks a million and one questions about their genetic history and heritage, I am reminded that they are not of my flesh and blood. I have been given them to steward until my job is finished. And then my heart hurts that they will someday have to navigate the complicated feelings of belonging and yet not belonging. They will have to face the deep, painful truth that they were given to us. *They were given away.* Given to us from someone they most likely will long to know. The sense of abandonment and rejection is there whether we want to acknowledge it or not. So instead of shying away from this and trying to ignore what will most likely become a huge part of them, I want to hold my hands open to their questions and their pain. The more we can allow the conversations and questions about their birth parents, the more hopeful I am that when they start to think about the bigger and harder questions, they will know Jon and I are a safe place. We will do our best to answer their questions and even help them discover what they want to know.

No, we're not naturally gracious and accepting of all this. This has been a journey of opening our eyes to a bigger picture than what we can see right now, of letting go of control and relinquishing to God's overarching omniscience. Has He ever given us something that His grace does not sufficiently cover? No. And beyond that, if we can truly allow our hearts to rest in the belief that he has gone before us, then our petty insecurities can die away and allow room for a beautiful conversation that each of our children needs in the deepest part of their soul. The conversation that allows them to be truly them. So, when my sweet daughter has crocodile tears streaming down her face because she misses someone she's never met, but still somehow *knows* them, I can set aside my jealousy and give her the enveloping hug she needs.

I could easily think about how I'm the one who zips up her princess costumes again and again, makes her crackers and cheese plates, bandages her scraped knees, and tucks her in tightly with her bunny and blankey each night, so why doesn't she have the same fervent emotions towards me? But that's not the real question is it? The real question sits within fear and tries to take hold of our hearts. It is: *Will they love me as their true parent or will they always mourn what they lost?* That is the scary question that keeps adoptive parents from disclosing personal details about birth parents to their adopted children. That is the reason so many adoptions used to be closed instead of open. And that is the reason your heart lurches when my child asks about their "real" mother. Are there some things that are too mature for their ears? Yes, most certainly. But in time those things will have to come into the light too. In time, everything I know, they should know too. It is only my fear of being replaced that could keep me hoarding away the details for myself. My unresolved sorrow that wishes her hair was like mine and not her birth mother's. My insecurities that they won't take after me or Jon, but instead their birth parents. It is *fear*. Fear of being rejected for the role we've chosen to play. Fear that someone will replace us and that our own child will choose to love someone else more than us. *Fear we will love and not be loved in return.*

And so we sit in that fear and choose to release it to God. The God who chose to love this world, knowing full well that many, many precious children of His would not return His love at all. But He chose to love us anyway. Our ability to love these children of ours *and* hold their tough questions in our hands, leaves room for challenging conversations, and is a direct reflection of the love God has shown to us.

So, back to *when* we tell our children. From the moment they are placed in our arms, their adoption story is part of them, part of who they are and part of our family. We tell their story with love and excitement. We do not fear what is ahead because we know, *we know*, that this is what God has planned for us and he forged the path by first loving us unconditionally. Our job is to hold the big crocodile tears and love their little souls the best we can.

22

Why We Will Never Retire

We sat outside in the warm California sun and entertained our toddler while waiting for the birth mother and her boyfriend. I knew the minute they appeared. Her slight, petite figure contrasted by his tall, strong athletic frame. Her long light brown hair and big almond eyes looked anxious as she glanced around looking for us. He seemed confident and comfortable as he walked next to her. I stood quickly to waive them over and her face lit up with a gorgeous smile, as did his. Her belly was small, tucked tightly into her small body. Just seeing it reminded me that that was possibly our baby in there. Then the nerves took over.

But this story starts a bit earlier than that. We arrived home with our first born, in awe of what had just transpired, in awe of the little baby we held in our arms. And then, we readied ourselves to prove to the state that we could keep her, and once again emptied our bank account to cover the final wave of expenses. This is the odd, gray area of adoption. We were adjusting to life with a new baby *and* juggling phone calls to the lawyer and state with their follow up questions. The birth mother had relinquished her parental rights, so technically we were the legal guardians of the baby, but the adoption would not be finalized for at least six months. In the middle of our newborn bliss, while we were cocooning ourselves from the outside world, we would have two more home visits to check in on us and make sure the state could endorse this adoption. In the middle of the sleepless nights, endless feedings, visits from well- wishers, we would be analyzed, poked and prodded.

With our first baby this process was intimidating, nerve racking actually. But as we came to realize, the hard work of proving ourselves had already been completed. These were just the final steps in the paperwork that needed to be completed before it could be submitted to the court. The expenses we needed to cover were the final fee to our lawyer (paid after the birth of the baby), and the last wave of birth mother expenses that would cover the costs of her living for the next six weeks. We were drained-financially, emotionally, and physically (hello newborn sleep schedule). The first time we weathered the weeks after a baby's birth felt like a slow marathon. Managing logistics, paperwork, fielding texts from the birth mother when all we wanted to do was sit quietly and enjoy our new baby. Not to mention, I was back to work, infant in tow, facing down a full wedding season of events. But we were grateful, oh-so grateful that God had carried us these last five months. He had provided financially. He had prepared us mentally and emotionally. He had prepared us for this new journey on which we were now embarking. Our job was to love this little human unconditionally and to the best of our ability.

And then 14 months later, we started all over again. A couple things never changed between each adoption. Every time we wanted to adopt we had to prove ourselves worthy and capable of being parents. And you know, after all that proving, I certainly don't think it helped us actually be better parents-it just made us a lot less confident about it.

We also had to repeat the blood tests, the dmv records, the physicals, the letters of recommendation, the home visits, etc. The only reason it got easier each time was that we knew the drill. Our friends saved their recommendation letters and faithfully sent them out each time. Our doctor made room in his schedule and happily signed the forms saying we were in good health. We knew where to go for fingerprinting and the hours they were open. Basically what I'm saying is that it got easier each time because we knew how to jump through the hoops-which is good, because the timeline for each adoption got faster.

This time, our lawyer could not meet with us for the initial meeting with the birth mother, but since this wasn't our first rodeo, we felt comfortable enough to meet her on our own. (Well, as comfortable as one can be on a blind first date where the question that is up for debate is, "Do I want to give you my child?"). Our lawyer had suggested that if we wanted to adopt again, we might expect to wait a bit longer for a match. In her experience most birth mothers would be interested in placing a child with a family who didn't have any children, blessing them with their first child. But that was not to be the case. Two weeks after we gave our portfolio to our lawyer, this couple had selected us. So here we were, driving down to Los Angeles once again, this time with a toddler in tow, to meet at an outdoor cafe in a plaza. We attempted a normal conversation trying to get to know everything we could about this birth mother and father.

We by now realized that unless we made the effort to ask the questions-getting to know their story, their history, their family, their life-those questions would not get asked. Not only would they not get asked, but then we might never know the answers. We wouldn't know that our second baby would be partially Hawaiian. Or that the birth mother loved and was studying anthropology and the birth father was 6' 4" and was a model in his spare time. We wouldn't know that her family fully supported her decision to place her baby. We wouldn't have found out that the main reason they liked us for their unborn baby is that he (yes, it was a boy) would have a sibling close in age, like she had experienced. The birth mother valued that sibling connection and had chosen us because we would be able to offer that gift to her child.

All the fears we faced with each adoption-whether they would change their mind or not-were pushed aside and the urgency to know these two lovely people the best we could took precedence. Did we still have fears and anxious thoughts? Of course. We are human after all and I have do have a highly active imagination. But, what we kept reminding ourselves as we chatted with them, is that this might be our only opportunity to memorize the color of his eyes, the slightly crooked way she smiled, and the shy laughter that would shake her shoulder. I think the hardest part of adoption is the unknown fears that creep in, and we were no longer afraid to ask questions on behalf of our unborn child. After all, as I have mentioned before, this child will want to know about their birth parents and each thing I can tell him will be a gift. This first meeting, this awkward first date, ended up being one of the only times we would get to ask questions and get to know this birth mother and father. The baby was born only a few weeks later and we would never see or hear from this couple again. God knew we needed boldness in this adoption. He knew we needed to have one experience under our belt so that we would know to learn all we could about these birth parents before the opportunity was lost on us.

This adoption was exactly what we had needed as well. For as much as the first adoption had been wrought with fears, conflicts, and surprises, this one was easy. *Easy.* We met, we loved them and they loved us.

She was a quiet spoken college student with a ready smile. Her big, gentle eyes communicated compassion and selflessness. If I've learned anything about birth mothers over the course of all these adoptions, it's that they're selfless. They're making a desperately hard decision on behalf of an unborn child. A decision that requires them to sacrifice their own desires over and over again. This birth mother was no different. Her situation and the trajectory of her life did not allow her to raise a child. Her thoughtfulness and openness was humbling. We left that meeting confident she was a good match for us, apparently she felt the same way too. So we completed all our needed documents and hoop jumping, and paid our fees. And because this all transpired faster than we thought it would, we were back to scrambling for the funding once again.

In the efforts to be as transparent as possible with you, this time we leveraged Jon's retirement-a decision most would advise against. But if you're allowed to leverage your retirement for a down payment, then why shouldn't you utilize it for building a family, which was endlessly more important to us than buying a house? We were happy to cram into our tiny 960 square foot, 2 bedroom, 1 bath rental cottage and live a full to overflowing life with two babies. We took the fact that Jon had retirement saved as a blessing to help us in this journey. Did we ever regret this decision? Well, in all honesty, yes. We have always used whatever means possible to help pay for our adoptions. We have used our savings, we have used our retirement, we have taken out a personal loan, we borrowed from our family, we have fund-raised. We've begged, pleaded, and humbled ourselves, and lived in rentals for years, *years*, so that we could pay the adoption costs associated with four kids. But any regrets we have are eclipsed by the glorious brightness that four children bring.

But, this financial strain is still the dirty little secret about private adoption that no one talks about. It's expensive and it is a huge financial sacrifice. We have never once regretted adopting four kids. Have four kids? Well, maybe sometimes. (I kid.) But adopting four kids? Never. However, sometimes we have looked around us at our contemporaries and seen their new homes, their remodeled kitchens, their open acreage, their sprawling house with a pool, their vacation home, their new cars, their fun vacations and we have swallowed our jealousy. Okay, maybe Jon has swallowed his jealousy-I most certainly have had (and sometimes still do) have to work through it with gnashing of teeth and pounding of fists. It is not that I am upset for my friends and their successes, it is more that we have had to sacrifice financially in order to build a family. Some people sneeze and they get pregnant, with their insurance covering everything but the co-pay for the birth. Some of us drain our retirement, savings, and good will of all their family and friends in order to bring a baby home, in order to build the family we have a vision for.

Those some of us (sheepishly raises hand) have to work through feelings of jealousy, resentfulness and discontentment, and build character instead. Oh yay. Has it been worth the cost? Was each child worth more than a full savings account? Absolutely. But see, this isn't just about adoption either. This is the comparison trap that so many fall prey to as the trajectory of their life takes them in a different direction than those around them. If we spend too much time looking around at what others have that we do not, we give ourselves the burden of discontentment. And discontentment is so sneaky, it is hard to weed it out from among the flowers that is your own life. One little tiny discontent seed sews itself in the form of thoughts like, *They were able to take a vacation this year, but we have to save for this other thing instead. I wish we could go on a vacation.* And now that little seed has taken root.

Then the next little thing comes along, *Did you see how they replanted their backyard? It is the perfect entertaining space now. It is so hard to only have grass and shrubs in ours. I wish we could have a nice entertaining space.* And another seed is sewn. Soon enough, the garden of your life is wrought with weeds taller than the beautiful flowers that had been in abundance, choking out the lives of each bloom you had been given. And when you look at your life, all you can see is weeds. We grew those weeds ourselves. We allowed the discontentment to grow and overtake our own blessings. We allowed ourselves to look around at others and envy what was growing in their garden.

So, the sooner I embraced (I still have to work on it), that the story God has for our life is different than others, the sooner I could let go of my envy. I could let go of whatever expectations I had for our life and embrace what He was laying before us. I could let go of the discontent. It is so much harder to do than to say, and like I have repeatedly claimed, its a constant mind battle. But the reward is so great. Living in the fullness of what you have been given, even if it is not what you expected-especially if it is not what you expected-allows you to open your hands to what God has intended instead. He is blessing you beyond your wildest imagination and it requires you looking up to see it, not around at others.

Up. Look *up*.

I look around and I see houses with spacious kitchens, gardens for entertaining, pools with pool houses, trips to Italy in the fall, and endless other desires of my heart in other's worlds. I look up and see these four precious lives that will be greater than any of my piddly desires. I look up and see God.

23

A Good Form of Self-Torture

We didn't look anything like them. I didn't see myself reflected in their eyes, hair, or skin color. On top of that, their cultural heritage was so different from ours. And yet, *and yet*, they had chosen us. And here we were, once again sitting across the table from a nervous birth couple who had selected our application out of all the others. We were surprised to have been selected, if I'm being honest. The first time we had put together our portfolio book, we looked appealing, if I do say so myself, a youngish couple, duel-income, loads of time to devote to a new baby. This time around I wasn't so confident in selling ourselves. Now we were in the "older parents" category, already two toddlers at home, dogs, chickens, cats-who was going to mind the new baby with all that was going on?

We were told they had been drawn to the full life (big family, traveling, lots of pets) we led, and could imagine their child in the midst of it. They were unfazed by our ages. But above all, we were floored to find out this baby would be fully Asian. Remember back when we were answering all the hard questions for the adoption application? How we were busy checking boxes for yes and no to all the possibilities?

124

Well, one box we had checked yes to was that we were okay with any race. We felt comfortable knowing that our diverse extended family, already full of color, would readily accept any race we adopted. But still we were surprised to find out that these Asian birth parents had selected us. What a gift that has turned out to be. Our daughter's heritage has opened our eyes to so many beautiful and lovely stories, traditions, and a broader world awareness. We rethought the way we approached children's books, movies, history, and cultural traditions. We became strategic with our community and where we live. Yes, living in a culturally diverse area was suddenly a high priority for us. It has been amazing.

So here we were in early February, meeting with this birth couple and to see if the match was right. Obviously you know that it was. They were lovely, kind, gentle, thoughtful people. I felt connected to the birth mother right away, despite all the obvious differences. And I know, because of Jon's history, the birth father knew we understood the pain of this situation for him. Our meeting with them was gentle and sweet. This time, however, we were not able to ask the 1 million questions blaring through my mind. They were very private people and our meeting was brief. I made plans to come back down to a doctor's appointment with the birth mother a couple weeks later and hoped that would allow us more time to get to know each other. Well, that didn't happen. Are you even surprised? You should know by now nothing ever goes according to plan.

We had just spent the night away at a lovely hotel for Jon's birthday. The stay had included massages, saunas, pool swims and a lovely dinner out. We were relaxed and rested. Jon headed home to take care of our two littles (ages 4 and 2), and I headed to Los Angeles for a wedding site visit. I had almost returned home that evening after driving two hours, when I received a call from the birth mother saying they were headed to the hospital. So I rushed home, kissed my babies goodnight, and Jon and I turned around and drove the two hours back down to Los Angeles. We had been told that the birth parents wanted privacy for this birth, so we were to wait nearby until we were invited into the room. We checked into a nearby hotel and waited.

And waited. And *waited*. I started to get anxious and was unable to sleep. It felt wrong to me to be so far away from "our" baby. I wanted to be there for her delivery, but we knew that it wasn't our choice. We then realized what a gift the first two birth mothers had given us by letting us be in the room during delivery. To see the first breaths of our babies, to hear their first cries. It should never be taken lightly how amazing it is to witness a birth. I kept hoping these birth parents would change their mind and message us to come to the hospital to join them. But that didn't happen. Hours went by as we tried to get some sleep at the nearby hotel. When they did finally contact us, it was to say she had been born two hours ago. I felt this mixture of joy and resentment. How could she already be born? I was here in this hotel room and she was over there in the hospital. I should be there holding her. I wanted to dash over there right away, even though it was 4 am. We were at the mercy of the birth parents and we needed to respect their wishes to remain private and alone. We needed to wait to be invited. So we sat in the hotel room and waited again.

Finally, later that morning around 9 am, we were invited over to the hospital room to hold our new baby. This time was so different from the previous two adoptions. We were not given a room with the baby in the hospital like before, instead, the birth parents wanted to keep her in with them. We were to stay down the street at the hotel and visit back and forth. And since our sweet baby girl was born at only 4 lb 6 oz, the hospital told us it might be a few days before she was released. She was perfectly healthy and formed, just tiny. The hospital wanted to make sure she was functioning just fine before releasing us. So the birth parents decided they'd stay with the baby in their room until all were released.

A tension started to build in us. You probably sense it too. My over-creative thoughts started to spiral. We felt so on the outside of this birth. We had spent the first day popping in for visits, completely subject to the hospital's visiting hours and the whims of the birth parents. My mama bear desire to hold this baby was kicking into high gear, but she wasn't yet my baby to hold. I wanted to feed her, change her, hold her close to my body. This was our third child now, and I knew how important those first few days of bonding were.

On top of this, when we did visit their room, we could feel the palpable pain and loss for both birth parents-their overwhelming sadness of the situation. We could see their internal struggle to hand over the baby for us to hold, change, and feed. So much so that Jon took this opportunity to speak to them about how he had been in their shoes, how hard the decision had been, and how he had known it was the best choice for his son. We tried to take these awkward visits as opportunities to get to know more about these lovely birth parents. We learned they both loved and had played classical music while growing up. They were both exceptionally smart and had a passion for cooking. While we held our new precious baby, we learned as much as we could about her heritage. Where she had come from and who she might become. As much as I longed to wrap her up and whisk her away to our safe home where her siblings awaited her, we made ourselves trust that God was in control and we took that faith and tried to make each hour spent with them an opportunity to love them, get to know them, and let them know how much we appreciated their decision to choose us.

The birth parent's desire to spend so much time with the baby fed those deep fears that were lurking, the fear they were going to change their minds. This adoption had been arranged through a colleague of our lawyer's, similar to our first adoption, so that facilitator was supposed to be our advocate. We did not see a soul from that office until the day we checked out of the hospital, despite many phone calls trying to seek their help and their insight on the situation. So we were alone in the hospital, advocating for ourselves and figuring it out as we went. If this had been our first adoption, we would have been terrified and panicking. Were they going to change their minds? We had no idea, but we did the best we could to assure ourselves that no matter what happened, we would be okay. What we failed to see in these few days was two parents making the hardest decision of their lives and mourning their choice, but knowing they still needed to carry it through. We were so focused on our on fears, we missed the opportunity to love these two birth parents in their pain.

What added to our tension and anxiety was that we had members of the hospital staff "take sides" on what they thought should happen. (This, of course, all happened in hushed tones and quickly silenced conversions when we walked by.) We learned over the course of the three days, when we were coming and going from their room, that many of the staff did not think the birth parents should place their baby with us. We had a few nurses who made it extra hard for us to be visitors during those visiting hours, almost being outright hostile towards us-as though we were doing something wrong. I see how they were trying to protect the best interests of the birth mother, but one nurse flat out asked the birth mother if she was being forced into this decision. Fortunately for us, the polarization of the hospital staff only drew us closer together with the birth parents. They shared the conversations they'd had with the nursing staff and how they had emphasized over and over again that this was their choice. They had *chosen* us. In the moment these conversations and situations were overwhelmingly intimidating. How do you walk through a hospital hall, passing nursing staff who know who you are, why you're there, and don't agree that you should be taking someone else's baby home? Looking back now, I realize how this was giving us the reassurance we needed-that this baby was designed for us, that we had been chosen by her birth parents, and that God's hand was still over all this.

Finally, after three tortuous days of coming and going from the hospital, we said our goodbyes and left with our new sweet baby girl. But that wasn't the end. Do you remember how I mentioned earlier the birth mother who didn't sign the paperwork relinquishing her rights, so technically she could change her mind within the first 30 days? Well that was this birth mother. So after all this, we still did not have that little piece of paper that gave us the 100% confidence that the baby was ours to keep. If you remember, it took two weeks for me to realize I was holding back from this sweet baby. Two weeks for me to be bold enough to ask once again if this birth mother was going to change her mind. And while she reassured us she wasn't, I didn't realize how relieved I was when the 30 days were up. It was as though a huge force had been lifted off my soul. I could let my shoulders relax, my breathing even out, and I could sleep again...well, as well as one can sleep when waking up every two hours to feed the tiniest human bean ever. Again, I was so focused on my own fears that I missed what this birth mother was not telling in her quiet way: that this was so hard for her, she was desperately trying to stay the course, but her heart was breaking. I could have used these conversations to connect with her more, to understand her a bit more knowing every little piece of her

I could gain would be a gift to my new baby. I could have loved her more, but I missed the opportunity as I was wrapped up in my own fears.

I feel like what I'm trying to emphasize here, is that no matter how many times we were to go through this process, no matter how many babies we were to adopt, it was never, never, lost on us how big a gift this was. The weight of someone else's painful decision that would then become the biggest blessing to us never lightened. It never became normal, regular, and business as usual. It always felt massively significant. It always felt as though the heavens had opened up and showered us with blessings in the form of a tiny, squirmy newborn. If I allowed fear to cloud my vision, I would not see beyond the storm clouds obscuring my vision, to the light beyond.

24

And Yet

My eldest child was launching herself down the slide upside-down and backwards, much to the dismay of the other playground parents, and my second-born was busily trying to climb the climbing wall, which was obviously much too big for him but that didn't seem to phase him at all. With one adventurous two-year-old and one very bold four-year-old, the newborn strapped to my chest seemed like an afterthought. She was by far the easiest one amongst this rabble. She started to get squirmy and so I gently removed the tiny 5 lb baby from the cocoon that enveloped her. As I did so, the mother next to me on the bench curiously peered over, as all mothers do when a newborn emerges, and did a double-take between this tiny baby in my arms, my face, and the two hellions out on the playground. Gingerly she asked, "Is she adopted?"

With the addition of this third child, regularly being on the receiving end of this question was new to us. Our other two children could easily be mistaken for biological children, especially our first who looked amazingly like I did as a child. But this third one had one hundred percent Asian heritage, which we do not share-not even a little bit. So wherever we went we were immediately asked a similar version of the same question. Clearly this child was not of our genes. I would always respond the same way, saving myself a long future explanation, "Yes, they all are." If I didn't clarify that my entire brood was adopted, I'd have to go through them hedging around asking after the other two, which clearly looked like they belonged. This third baby clearly did not.

So once I had divulged our non-traditional family make-up, I braced myself for what was next. First, there would be raised eyebrows, then a thoughtful pause, a big breath, and then our conversation would take one of two vulnerable directions: A). "I have always wanted to adopt…"then cue all the excuses justifying why they hadn't, apparently fielding some imaginary judgment against them (I promise not by me). Or B). "Wow. I could never do that." And then suddenly a cavern of astonishment would open up between us, as though adoption might be catching and if they stay too long they might unwittingly end up with some children. If any children were present, both conversations transpired in hushed tones with furtive glances in the directions of the children. The unspoken question of "Do they know?" filling their eyes. This whole interaction repeats itself so regularly that I am convinced our society has some pretty misinformed preconceived notions about adoption.

First off, it's not catching. By asking me questions about our children and adoption you will not suddenly end up with a pile full of children filling your minivan. I'm sure our story has already proven how purposeful you have to be in adoption. How nothing just "happens" and even it seems like it does, God has clearly gone before you, and so you can trust the outcome. Secondly, and I've mentioned this before, yes, our children know. So I'm quick to anticipate this question and disclose that since they were been brought home from the hospital they have been told their stories over and over again. We are proud of their stories, their heritages, and how we came to be their parents. We consider them huge blessings and don't hesitate to tell them so.

But that's not really the most important part of these conversations, it's not really what people are expressing with their raised eyebrows and closer examination of our family, as they run their own scenarios through their heads. What they are really expressing is fear. The fear of the unknown. *I've always wanted to adopt, but I don't think I could do it.* Then cue 100 different excuses, most coming from a fear of the unknown. *How would we pay for it? What if we don't get chosen? How would it affect our biological children? My partner doesn't want to and every time we discuss it they shut it down.* These fears are real, but not based in faith, which is of course the only reason we have been able to adopt over and over again. We both had faith that God would walk this journey with us each time-open the doors that needed to be opened, making the connections, and providing the finances. We were willing to open our hands up to be parents to those who needed parents, and we were trusting He would provide for us. But faith aside, the fears we have about adoption come from the many, many failed stories we hear. The heartbreak, the disappointment, the financial mess. I'm hoping, if anything, that our story proves you can have all those things: heartbreak, disappointment, financial mess *and yet* still have a beautiful story. The *"and yet"* is the most important part of most stories. It's actually what makes a story. The "despite all odds" part of the story is what makes you want to tell it over and over again. If we could only approach adoption like we do other big decisions in our lives, the fear would lessen and faith would take its place.

Just go with me for a bit. You want to buy a house. You've never purchased one before, but you know you want one. So what do you do? You ask other people who have already purchased houses how to start. You ask around to enough people and eventually a pattern emerges. You never fear that if you ask too many questions you might just end up with a house plopped in your lap. The "how" starts to feel less vague and more attainable. So you start to look around at your options and you make a list of things you love and want in a house. Then you start to figure out what you can afford. You don't wait until you're making an offer on a house to figure out what you can afford or what you like, you do it before you even start touring houses (or you should, if no one has told you this yet). You should figure out what you can afford before you start getting attached. Then you do what everyone does-tour houses and fight over the merits of each house. You like this one, but your partner likes that one. Then, you finally come to a compromise, you leverage all you have, make an offer and jump ship! Yay! Now you really start to freak out over what you just did. Adoption is very similar, no joke.

The process needs to be looked at with an objective point of view *first*. If the thoughts of adoption (positive or negative) have crossed your mind more than once, then you don't need to even consider "I want to" or "I don't know if we can" adopt. You need to look at it objectively first and see why you keep returning to it. I'm a big believer that God places small seeds in our hearts along our journey, like He did with mine, preparing us for a bigger and better plan ahead.

I've walked through how my story led me to adopt four children, but what is in your story that has placed this desire (or at the very least, curiosity) on your heart? My suggestion is that you walk through the logic first. There are simple logistics that come prior to your decision to adopt that can be addressed and discussed neutrally. Do we have room in our house for children or would we have to move? Do we have the freedom and finances to take care of them? Do we have other children and how would everyone assimilate? Do we have the finances (or the potential finances) we can leverage to help us fund the adoption. I already told you we leveraged our retirement to help us fund some of our adoptions. The options are there; you just have to review your situation neutrally before getting too attached to either "We can't do it" or "I want to do it." And once you have objectively analyzed your situation, now open your hands to the *and yet* part of your story.

Which part of your objective review feels rough? At which part does the hesitation sneak in? For us it was finances. Our hearts were ready, our minds were prepared to tackle the challenges and let go of preconceived ideas, but the finances were a huge emotional battle for us. Most likely because they were tight and we would had sacrifice comforts in order to fund our adoptions. But that has also been the exact area God has used over and over with each adoption to surprise us with His provision. When we didn't know where that next few thousand would come from, there it was either through an unexpected job or a gift from a friend. For you, the struggle might be you're not sure how your other children will adjust to an adopted sibling. Or, you might fear that you'll be the story that ends in heartache as the birth mother decides to keep the baby. Whatever the fear is that is keeping you from adoption, this is your opportunity prove to yourself that you have a faith bigger than that. Those fears can be laid at God's feet, and He will give you and your family the resources you need to bring a precious child home. He will give you the faith you need to push past the heartbreak and struggles.

So every time someone asks me if my children are adopted, I look at it as an opportunity to extinguish the fears they are holding onto.

Yes sure, not everyone who asks is interested in adopting, but most still cling to the scary stories they've heard and retell them whenever adoptions comes up. So I take it upon myself to breathe inspiration into those curious hearts. If not for them, then for their friend, or their sister, or the next time someone mentions adoption. Next time, they will have a better story to tell than heartbreak. I want to tell our story with the financial struggles, the disappointments, and all the way to the *and yet* part of our story. *And yet* there was extreme beauty. I want to replace fear with a faithful hope.

25

Secret Scary Questions

The candles were softly glowing. Forks and knives sat discarded on top of of empty plates, napkins tossed carelessly aside. The wine bottle was being passed up and back down the table as glasses were refilled and each guest pushed back from the table a bit to settle into the evening of good conversation over a shared meal. Legs propped up on knees, arms gently around backs of chairs, the soothing Spanish guitar music drifting around our ears. Then, without fail, a hushed question from a pensive and thoughtful husband whose inhibitions had been loosened by the wine. "How do you know you will love them as much as you would a biological child?" Suddenly you could hear a pin drop and the background Spanish guitar seemed way too loud. All eyes were on me and I could feel my heart start to race. *I didn't know. How was I to know? I hadn't even met the child yet (but really, is that good logic anyway?)* But here is what I have *learned.*

There is one conversation that comes up over and over again when I speak to one partner in a relationship-the "my partner does not want to adopt" conversation. This sneaks its way into conversations more often than I'm comfortable with. According to my very unofficial, not very balanced survey, it seems like half of the people I talk to say this. How can half of society just not want to adopt at all? What did we do to make it so scary and dark that people have such an aversion to it? We definitely don't feel the same way about dog and cat adoptions. People throw themselves at those and sometimes a bit too readily. (You're thinking, "How can you even compare pet adoptions to child adoptions?" Well, you can't really...except for if you'd had a toddler, then you sort of can.)

This comes from the same fear as a question that is often whispered in the secret places that scary adoption questions are whispered: "How do you know you'll be able to fully unconditionally love this child who is not of your flesh and blood?" This question usually creeps out after a glass of wine (or two), in the corner of the kitchen when no one else is listening-or in the quiet voice of a mother on a playground who would love to adopt but is afraid her love will not be equal to that of her biological children. It comes from the same place as "My partner doesn't want to adopt." Sometimes it's voiced as, "I don't think I could love someone else's child."

I want to be clear that there is no shame in voicing this question. Just as there is no shame in asking yourself how you can fall in love. How you are able to commit to someone for life in marriage? You do it by *choosing* to. We assume that a child who is of your own flesh and blood will be more natural to love than one who is not. But why would we assume this? Is it because we love ourselves so much that any person who comes from us must be the most lovable of all? Or perhaps we love someone else so much that any being that is produced by them is the most lovable thing we've ever met? Once we say it out loud it sounds ridiculous, doesn't it? Take a red-eye flight together and suddenly your significant other doesn't feel so great anymore. If anyone should know that we are not the most deserving of unconditional love, it's us. And the more time we spend loving (or traveling with) the person we have chosen to love, the more we see their faults, am I right?

Our English vocabulary limits love to one word. And unfortunately, this one little word holds so many different meanings and nuances that trying to wrap your head around loving someone-how it's possible to fall in love, or innately love a child, or choose to love someone again and again over is nearly impossible. How can each of these situations be the same love? Well, because they're not. The Greeks broke the concept of love into seven different types (sometimes eight-it depends on which dead Greek you're talking to), each being distinct in their characteristics. Before we had adopted our first child, I didn't know how to answer the questions posed to me about how I was going to love this child. But now, after experiencing this amazing phenomena again and again, I have a better understanding of what they are actually asking and how to answer. When someone asks me "How do you know you'll love a baby who is not your biological child?" we need the Greek definitions of love to break down exactly what they're asking.

Science may prove that a biological connection is strong, but then how do you explain all the people who love their spouses, their friends, or even someone else's family more than they love their own? Because it is a choice. This is *agape* love-a selfless, sacrificial love. I can already hear your protests: it's easy to choose the person we feel in love with. Yes, that is because what came first was *eros* love. The love that is passionate, filled with desire …and obsession. And did you know that if you were sustained on only *eros* love you'd go crazy? It releases too many chemicals to your brain-dopamine, serotonin and oxytocin, to be precise. And if we were to only have *eros* love, these euphoric chemicals would become like a drug to us and eventually we would enter into the imbalanced love of *mania* (obsessive and toxic love). So eventually, we have to move past that first attraction and hot, sexy love into something more sustainable. We have to choose to love them. Unconditional love is a choice and it is a choice you make daily. Sometimes it is easy, sometimes it is not. But you continue to choose to love. And, as anyone with a toddler will tell you, you will have to continue to choose to love as a parent at great sacrifice to your sanity.

Loving a biological child may seem more natural because there are familiar characteristics woven into their being-things you expect to see or hope to see. The expectation that you will unconditionally love them is unspoken, they are of you after all. You brought them into this world; it is your responsibility to love them no matter what. But as we learn a child, letting them unfold in who they are, we are surprised by who they become-they are their own person, after all. They may have your smile, but that personality and temperament came out of left field. Or they may have your attitude but they look nothing like you. An adopted child presents an opportunity for both the child and the parent. We have to learn the child as their own being. There is no opportunity to superimpose on them any familiar characteristics. Our opportunity to learn each of our children for who they are and who God designed them to be is a gift to them. When our perspective of who they are is not shrouded by "You are just like your Grandma Becky." (although she is wonderful, and I'd love to be like her) or "You have your Dad's laugh," we are learning and loving each child as an adventure.

It is like reading a good character in a book, uncovering each layer of who they are as each chapter passes. Yes, there is honor and sometimes blessings in inherited characteristics, passed from one generation to another. But sometimes there is also pain or shame in inherited characteristics and a child does not have the opportunity to be a different person from those before them until they are aware enough to insist differently. Often this only occurs when we are well into adulthood and have to undo all the preset assumptions of us. With adopted children there are none of these expectations to become a certain way. With adopted children you *choose* to love them first and then are surprised by the joy of who they are as you learn them. You fall in love with them as they unfurl their petals.

Unconditional love is as much a choice with biological children as it is with adopted children. Your ability to choose to love them is *agape* love. A love that allows them to be who they are and give them unrestricted absolute love, so they in turn can relax into themselves and flourish. We are all capable of giving others this love. It is no different with a child-yours or someone else's-the difference is allowing yourself to choose. Once you choose to love someone unconditionally, you allow yourself to set aside preconceived expectations of who they might become and embrace who they are. With biological children, it is assumed we will do this, so we do without much thought. With adopted children it is a conscious choice. So, back to the lurking secret question: how do I know I can love them unconditionally?

Because I choose to and will continue to choose to for as long as I live.

26

Greek Matters

B ut let's address another side of love that is often mistaken for unconditional love-the instinct to shelter and protect. In Greek this is *storge* love, or familial love. This is the love that is natural, instinctual and doesn't expect anything in return. It is the tenderness you give someone when you want to make them feel comfortable and safe. We need to separate the choice of unconditional love (agape) from the devoted feelings of intuitively needing to safeguard someone or provide for them a secure environment. This love is intuitive, subtle, and a bit more primal. It is without saying that when a helpless newborn is placed into your arms under your care, you have an instinct to protect them. And when a helpless newborn is actually *given* to you, well that instinct kicks up about 1000 percent. Well, at least it was for me. My mothering instincts kicked into high gear the minute I became responsible for each child. It was absolutely different from holding a friend's newborn. My entire being felt responsible for them. I would do absolutely anything to protect them, to provide for their needs, and to shelter them from harm. My need to know them and protect them was intuitive and instinctual from the beginning.

But that is not the case with everyone. Sometimes your primal instinct to shelter and protect needs a bit of time to develop. Sometimes it does feel like you're holding someone else's child. But candidly, some biological parents feel this way as well. And well, honestly, this was Jon. And no one we know would say that he loves our children with less fierceness than I do. But it just took him longer to allow himself to feel the primal instinct to shelter and protect this new little being. Did it mean he shouldn't be a parent? Did it mean that he was a bad parent?

No, it did not mean nor does it mean you are a bad parent, or you shouldn't be a parent, it simply means your natural desire to primally protect someone other than yourself is down a little deeper. It needs a bit more coaxing to get out. Self-protection and self-preservation have us guarding ourselves like crazy and we need to relax into our propensity to care for others. We have been far removed from the basic fight or flight environment and are so protected from most threats, that the primal instinct to care for someone else has been tamped down. Having children will bring this inclination to the surface, but sometimes we have to get past our own fears first.

This instinct to protect and sacrifice is to become vulnerable, to lay yourself bare before someone else, because this *storge* love needs to be given without any expectations. It is the desire to care for someone regardless of whether or not they can love you back and that is always scary. This is the side of love that is protective, selfless, and self-sacrificing. When I point out this instinctual type of love, most people understand it would be natural to care for an adopted child-of course they could and would be able to dig into this deep-seated instinct to protect and provide. But that still doesn't answer the unsettling question nagging at the back of their mind.

Then there is one other type of love, and I think this is what people are actually asking when they ask "How do you know you'll love them?" In Greek, this is *ludus* love, or simply, playful and enjoying love. This is also the side of love that brings great pleasure and affection. In a romantic relationship, this is the love that everyone looks forward to. The love that comes before the *eros* or sexual love. It's the flirting, the enjoyment of each other, the "time flies when we're together" love. *ludus* love gives us a bunch of hormones, such as dopamine and serotonin, which allows us to feel euphoric and addicted to the object of our affection.

I'd like to suggest that this love exists between a parent and a child as well. In a parent/child relationship, this is the side of love that delights in your child, takes pleasure in them. This explains that rush of attachment and "in love" feeling parents have for their newborn. This is the trickiest love to explain in adoption. I bet you can see how unconditional *agape* love (choice) and *storge* love (instinctual need to protect and provide) for a child are not much different between biological children and adopted children. However, this last love-cherish, adore, infatuated, take pleasure in-is the hardest to describe. Here's why: it comes loaded with guilt. This is the part no one wants to admit they're scared of. Of course you should enjoy your child. Of course you should take pleasure in their existence. Of course you should adore them. But what happens if you don't? What happens if you bring this tiny newborn home and you don't "love" them the way you thought you would? This is the part of love that feels like a roller coaster. If unconditional love is a choice and instinctual love is vulnerable and fierce, this love is devious and like water through your hands. One minute it's there and you're thriving in it, then the next minute you don't understand what happened. Our expectation is that we will feel this pleasurable, playful, enjoying love all the time with our new baby. All. The. Time.

But we will not. Nor should we be expected to. And this is where the guilt comes in. Because we chose to adopt, because we were given the responsibility to love and care for these children, and because someone gave us their child, we should "love" them all the time, right? Well, yes, we should-unconditionally (*agape*) and with a protective fierceness (*storge*). But we will not always enjoy them. Just as a biological parent will not always enjoy, take pleasure, and adore their child. There is no reason to feel guilty about this either. We were not designed to be on an endless pleasure journey in our lives, constantly living on a high of hormones and serotonin, only tolerating things and people that bring us pleasure.

This is why in romantic relationships we move past the flirting, playful love of *ludus* into something deeper for a lasting relationship. Is the *ludus*, playful, enjoying love gone? No, we are just deepening it with other types of love. We were designed to be loyal, steadfast, and sacrificial because we chose to love someone. I feel that in adoption, your choice to love comes first, *storge* love follows quickly as you see the child's need to be sheltered, protected and cared for, and then *ludus* love comes as a surprise in the most unexpected places. The first smiles of a newborn. The laughter of an infant. The joy of who they are becoming. All this allows you to take pleasure in them. The pleasure, enjoyment, and cherishing of each child grows and changes as they grow and change. Just as no one has stayed "madly in love" (*eros* love, for those keeping track in Greek) for endless years, you cannot be expected-I cannot be expected-to always feel madly in love with my child. Therefore, release yourself of that expectation. I'm working on it too.

Once we had released ourselves from false expectations and instead embraced that unconditional love of which we knew we were capable, it was easy to love each of our children from the moment they were placed in our arms. We gave ourselves permission to feel the other loves (*storge* and *ludus*) more slowly-allowing ourselves to get to know this new little person, just as you might a new friend. Most biological parents feel like they "know" their child from the moment they are born, and maybe that is true. Or maybe that is what we tell ourselves to help us along in the journey. After all, parenting is hard and we need all the help we can get. However, I'd like to suggest that each child, adopted and biological, is a new little creation that is waiting to be learned. Our love for them will only grow as we get to know them. As we see the same little quirky smile after every belly laugh. As we see the way they tuck their head into the nook of your neck when they're nervous. As we watch them unfold into a little human our desire to love them in all the ways will grow and grow.

So, to answer the question prowling around in everyone's mind: yes, you can-and you will-love any adopted child more than you can possibly imagine. Differently than with a biological child as your choice to love comes first-but doesn't that just make it all the more powerful? You will choose to love them long before you meet them. You will continue to choose to love them for as long as you live. And that child will be forever blessed because you continued to choose them.

That is a powerful love.

27

The Gift We Gave Our Children

I'm standing in the grocery store near-but not yet in-the checkout lines, close enough that I can feel the cashier's eyes on me. My cart is full to overflowing with boxes of cereal, cans of beans, jugs of milk, loaves of bread, fruits of all kinds, and random items one of my four children snuck into the cart when I wasn't looking. Currently, I can barely concentrate on anything else outside of the four small voices each asking, "May we please get..." and "Why can't we have...?". Not one of them reaches higher than my shoulder, but for some reason their limbs seem to be ages long as they reach for everything. A couple are hanging off the cart, threatening to tip the entire precariously loaded thing over. The other two are darting back and forth between the shelves and the cart thrusting items so close to my face I can't read the labels, asking over and over again, "Can't we *please* just get this...?"

Of course, this is when the dapperly dressed, older gentlemen with the hand basket containing a mere two items and a bundle of flowers for some deserving love, leans in towards me, as though about to reveal a great secret, and says, "You have your hands full, don't you?"And then flashes me a sympathetic smile that conveys how nice he is to notice my predicament-that perhaps I did not chose for myself, but was instead thrust into-and boy does he feel sorry for me. I barely manage to acknowledge him with a tolerant smile, for sure noting how different our worlds must be, before another item is thrust so close to my face it hits my nose. And then it is back to wrangling my small smugglers before facing the nerve-wracking check out line where I'm forced to bag my groceries while trying to prevent small hands from tangling in other passing carts all while carrying on a pleasant conversation with the checker. And you know what? This was not the only time I found myself on the receiving end of this same exact phrase. No, this would (and still does) happen every time I go out with my four children. Every. Time. And each time, the deliverer of the line acts as though this was probably the first time *anyone* has *ever* told me that.

This is the part of the story that pushes it over the top for most people. They can understand wanting a family. They can understand adopting a child or two. They can even understand adding a third to the mix, especially after they meet our third and are charmed by her. But a fourth? Someone has lost it. Someone has gone off their rocker. Someone is taking more than their fair share of life. Four children is a *large* family, and tips you over on the scales from "nice" family to "big" family. You have no choice but to enter into the large-family-vehicle club. The two-hotel room vacations. The special line reserved for chaotic families with way too many bags at airport security. Hosts' eyes widen at restaurants when you ask for a table for six-four children please. People comment every time you're out and about with all of them-usually something charming like, "Wow, aren't you busy?" or "Are they all yours?"

Four children is a lot. There are never enough ears to hear all the words that need to be said. Never enough space for people to truly be alone.

Hardly enough time to give each child the individual attention they deserve. And no matter how hard we try, it doesn't seem like there is enough of us to go around. And by now you all know it wasn't an accident. We didn't just get pregnant and oops, we have four! No, we chose this deliberately. And why would you chose-and even pay for all this chaos? If four children are so hard, why do it? (Jon asks himself this every day). So why, *why*, did we choose it?

We chose this for them. We wanted to give our children the gift of each other. We wanted to surround them with other stories like their own, purposefully creating a large family around their unique circumstances. This is no judgment towards people who chose to adopt just one or even two children. Adoption is hard. It is hard for both the adoption parents *and* especially for the children. In the future they will face a lot of difficult questions and need all the support they can get. This was a choice we could make so we did. As much as four children is fun and wild, it's also exhausting. It's expensive. It's hard. It's exactly everything everyone said it would be. And yes, I do have my hands full, thank you very much.

But at the heart of it, it is not about us, it's about *them*. It is about what we could give these children. We made the conscious decision from the start to build a family around adoption. We did not always plan on having four children, and if I'm completely transparent, sometimes we are overwhelmed by our own choices. But again, we have continually made decisions with our children in mind. We believe God gifted us with the strengths, talents, and the means He did so that we could provide for these children-to build a life for them that we think will bless them, like most parents strive to do. Our choices just look a bit different than others.

Each child brings to our lives-and to the lives of their siblings-joy, companionship, camaraderie, understanding, compassion, and love. We thought to ourselves, the more people they have in their corner as they grow and uncover their stories, as hard as those stories might be, the better it will be for each of them. Imagine having a group of close friends all with similar origin stories, how encouraging that would be when facing the ins and outs of life, navigating the nuances that your history lays over all your life. You would feel a deep sense of bonding over the simple fact you all came from similar backgrounds. It would be harder to feel alone. Most likely, someone would be aware of your well-being and be looking out for you. We wanted to give that to our children.

Yes, we could have stopped at two giving them each other. We could have gone on after those two children to purchase our first house or save for their college funds. But no, we took that third down payment and built a bigger clan for our children. Then finally, we took all our savings again and committed to a fourth child. We sacrificed some of the dreams we had as a couple to follow the internal nudging of God that told us to create a large tribe, a more substantial family. And we work hard everyday to help them be lifelong friends with each other. We want them to be each other's people. As they write each of their stories, we want their siblings to be their biggest fans and their best audiences. Besides, remember how we are "older" parents? We won't always be here for them. So, we gave them each other.

28

How to Be Miserable in Your Fairy Tale

Etta was just about one year old, and I finally had an evening off from client meetings. I had been busy for a couple weeks straight with back-to-back evening meetings as the spring season of weddings ramped up. Jon had been pulling the extra weight doing Etta's evening routine each night while I was out. Then one evening I finally was home. I so looked forward to holding my baby, giving her her last evening bottle as she fell asleep in my arms. It was always one of those moments I treasured because it nourished that dream I'd held onto since I was a child. So I went to prep the bottle for the evening feed and my husband stopped me by saying, "She doesn't take a bottle anymore."

I'm sorry, what? She doesn't take a bottle anymore?

I had missed the last evening holding my sweet baby until her eyes grew heavy and her small hands let go of the bottle, because I was out with clients. I still cry when I think about this.

Fast forward to three children later and the daily world hadn't slowed at all, but only become increasingly more full. Our schedule consisted of seeing Jon off to work, walking to the nursery down the street from our house to drop off the children, then I would return home to work on proposals, ordering flowers, and meeting with clients while sipping a lovely warm cup of coffee. On the way to the nursery, we would stop by my parent's house to say good morning and share breakfast, or a second breakfast, as was the case with my children. Most days I would retrieve all three children around noon from the nursery, make the walk back home, stopping again by my parents to let the children run wild in the garden while I shared stories with my mother, my father joining in now and then. And then home for lunch and nap and quiet time with all the littles. During their rests, I would tackle more work, prep dinner and wait for Jon to arrive home to relieve me from the complaints and whining of the three children under four, who were swarming. After the chaos of bedtime, I would often return to editing proposals, placing flower and supply orders, and basically not relaxing.

This was a lovely, calm pattern we had until Wednesday, then the second half of the week, I would work like crazy on whatever wedding we had that weekend. My team (including two sisters and my mother) would all descend upon our workshop at our house. The two older children would be whisked off to a babysitter for those days, I would wear the baby in the carrier, and I would not stop moving for what seemed like 48 hours. I would be dead on my feet come Friday night. Jon would come home from work, pick up the kids, make dinner, hand me a cocktail and then I'd collapse on the floor, too tired to even stand. Then I'd wake up, strap the baby to me and spend all day Saturday setting the wedding, and often, returning in the late hours of the night to clean up the wedding. Then Sunday I was too tired to move. Literally physically and mentally exhausted. It was a full thriving season, surrounded constantly by flowers, my small children, and family. Then the pandemic happened and our world stopped. Literally.

One day we were working up a storm and the next day we weren't. One day we had a schedule and routine for our family and the next day we didn't. I'm sure you've heard (or experienced) countless stories that sounded just like this. One minute your world is tumbling in one direction and suddenly everything stops. It was jarring, confusing, complicated, and a gift. I had been steadily building a career for which I had a vision. A vision of multiple weddings each weekend, my teams going out and managing each while I jumped between them. Having influence with local growers due to the sheer volume of floral we needed, and having influence with venues because we were there working so often. Creating a business that was respected and admired. Creating a name for myself. I was thriving. Then it all stopped. Suddenly I found myself at home all day, everyday, with three children under four and I hated it. Hated it. This dream I had longed for and prayed for for years and I hated it.

Then God began working.

Well, that's not really fair to Him because, actually, He was always working laying the groundwork for all this. But I think when our world stopped and I suddenly felt place-less, emotionally distraught, and not sure what the path forward looked like, I saw His hand. His hand was slowing me down, helping me see the beautiful life we had created for ourselves and our children. He was showing me how the trajectory of the life I was building was going in the opposite direction of what was good and true. I was seeking a name for myself, prestige, and money. When we were suddenly forced to stay home all day everyday and I was out of work for almost a year, we had to learn new routines, learn how to live with each other in the slowness-more than just tolerate, but thrive. We had to refocus our priorities and I had to be reminded of the earlier prayers that I had prayed so desperately and God had answered.

At first we were miserable, correction, *I* was miserable. I had moved so far away from my young self who had dreamed of being a mother. Now I wanted to be the mother who had lots and lots of help carrying for her children while she worked. I loved working. Loved. Loved the inspiring client meetings that required a sophisticated wardrobe. I loved the planning lunches with colleagues that usually involved wine. I loved the flower pick up days driving between farms and wholesalers loading our van full of fresh flowers. I loved the long quiet days (when the children were off at the nursery) sipping coffee and plunking away at the computer. I loved my freedom, my autonomy, and my identity in my career. I loved that I had a solid reputation and our services were in demand. I loved knowing that I had built all this and was on an upward trajectory for success.

And then suddenly I was thrust into a never-ending cycle of snacks, diaper changing, and little whining voices. I was suddenly always covered in sticky finger prints and stuck wearing the same black leggings and tank top combo every day. I felt myself spiraling into the fear that this was my future and I didn't want it. I wanted the controlled calm and not this noisy chaos.

But hold up. Didn't I just convince you of how hard we strived to create this life? This full-to-overflowing space filled with young children we had worked hard for? This was motherhood, why didn't I love it? Because at war within my soul was the narrow focus of what I had spent years cultivating as a career-building this family-run business that was beautiful and life-giving versus the desires God had placed in our hearts years before: the desire to have a family anchored in strength and love, unyielding in devotion to each other, and *time* together to build these things. Our current route was threatening this vision and we didn't even see it happening around us until everything stopped.

One day, while sitting in my parent's garden about six weeks after the pandemic shut down the world, my children were running wild and free and I was complaining, yet again, about feeling trapped. My mother simply said, "You will rise to the occasion. You always do. You will find it in you to enjoy the life God has planned for you." And it was in that moment, with the sunlight streaming through the trees, sitting with my mother, watching my children run wild, that I saw what our life could be-what I had hoped for my children when we adopted each of them-a safe, free life, full of joy with parents who were fully present and loved them deeply above all else. The path that I had unwittingly started on, which in all honestly had actually allowed us to afford these adoptions, was not actually the life I pictured deep down for them. I wanted to create a home that they could always come back to, feel unconditional love and acceptance, and understand that no matter what happened in their lives, they would have us, and that they were the most important things in our lives. Not a life where their mother was too busy juggling client demands to see the painting being presented to her by small hands. Not one where, as they grew into their new emotions as they matured, I dismissed them because I was so focused on the next flower order. Not one where the nanny went to the Mother's Day Tea held by the preschool because I had a wedding to prepare for (that may or may not have actually happened, and I still cringe thinking about it).

I needed to be present, fully present, to raise these children in the way that God had set before me. So in those nine months that we were forced to stay home and California was closed to all events, I relaxed into the vision God had for us: a slower life, full of time together, where my axis was our family and the floral work I did would be secondary. Hear me again when I say this: my career was not wrong, working is not wrong, having dreams of building a successful business is not wrong, having help so you can do these things is not wrong-but I had my priorities all mixed up. I had put my career and dreams first, not my children. When all our priorities shifted, they were distilled down to only the most basic things-being together, being with our extended families, being outside, gardening, eating and cooking nourishing foods, and immersing ourselves in God's desires for our life. Did the whining and endless snacks still bother me? Most certainly. And they still do. But I had an inner peace underlying it all saying this is where I needed to be right now.

29

One More to Go

I was taping roads in the patches of sunlight on our sealed cement floors for the cars that Wills had piled in my lap. Etta ran in circles around me with her pink sparkly fairy wings flapping to the princess mix-up music blasting through the speakers, while tiny Bianca was half-crawling around the living room putting everything she could find in her mouth. The fall day was warm, the cement floor cool, and the butterflies could be seen fluttering around the flowering anemones through our huge plate glass windows. The memory stands out as a typical afternoon in our new quiet pace. It was peaceful and chaotic as only life with small children could be as they asked for snacks for the thousandth time, and it was deeply soothing to my tired soul.

As our epidemic-lock-down-stay-at-home year progressed, I realized that my slower life was actually fulfilling the vision we had first had for our family. Now I realize you hear this all the time-slowing down is the key to living-stop rushing for more and embrace what is in front of you. And you're probably thinking I was stupid not to recognize it earlier. Sure, yes to all those things. But I loved working. LOVED it. I thrived in my work setting and it was so deeply fulfilling. However, my work life, my passion, my career had taken over and run the show. It was dictating our life's pace and pattern. It was like warm water coming to a slow boil. You adjust to the pace, then it picks up more, and you adjust again, then it picks up more, and you adjust again. Until you look back and realize that how you are living is not at all how you planned. And not until we were forced to slow down did I see it in our life.

The days of unrushed mornings with endless amounts of cereal served, rock and acorn discovery walks, playing music for a video dance party, and soaking in these three small children was not lost on me. Of course it was hard, there were three children under four and the first few months of our forced home stay, I was beside myself with how to manage. I was not used to being home and being in demand all the time. I collapsed many many times in tears, telling Jon that I was never meant to be home all the time with children. I kept trying to come up with plans to continue working, my entrepreneur brain working overtime to solve my problem.

Then I stopped fighting it. I stopped trying to push my agenda forward and I (once again, how many times do I need to learn this lesson?) listened to the inner prompting that was telling me to stop. Be slow. Let the days unfold before me without a to-do list or a plan. Absorb these children and this gift of time with my husband (who was of course home all the time now too). And so I did. I fought my own mind to keep it from racing ahead with plans. I let the slowness become my rhythm. We had tea parties, kiddy pool swims, bug collecting, cooking experiments, and lots and lots of tantrums. And I loved it-well, except the tantrum part.

As we did finally settle into this slower pace of life, I kept feeling like one last child was missing. We felt the pull towards one more. To me there was a balance in even numbers of children. Pairs, if you will. I had grown up with pairs of siblings and really enjoyed how there was always someone to be your buddy and technically there wasn't any "middle" child. My older sister and I were super close growing up. She always looked out for me and I was always faithfully following her around being her biggest fan. My youngest sister, the fourth one, was my "charge". Whenever we all went somewhere together I was responsible for looking out for her and my older sister was responsible for the third sister. Then these sisters developed the most beautiful friendships in high school and college. I loved these dynamics and wanted to give these to my children as well. There was something about giving these children, who may have been only children in another life, the gift of siblings. The gift of built-in friends and advocates. Besides, every amazing storybook about children has four kids, right? Two girls and two boys.

One day, on an unusually hot early winter day, after about nine months of not working, living a slower pace of life, and embracing the craziness that is three small children, our lawyer called to say she knew of a birth mother who would be having a baby boy in February. I was excitedly pacing our small backyard lawn, avoiding the chickens who were pecking lazily in the hot sun and unconsciously observing that the roses were still blooming, as she explained the situation. If you recall from the earlier stories, the previous adoptions all had challenges and almost broke us financially, so I was nervous about this next one. A year without me working had definitely left a mark, but we knew, we just *knew*, that God had one more for us and that He had already worked out all the details-including the always complicated and stressful finances.

So as I paced the lawn avoiding chickens, our lawyer confidently described how simple this adoption would be. You see, she had worked with this birth mother before, this baby would be the sixth child this birth mother would place for adoption. I bet you anything your first thought is *she must be doing this for the money*. But actually no, she wasn't. She refused most of all of the money offered to her. Her own story was one of childhood pain and loss. Of longing to feel connected and have a sense of belonging. She understood the weight of her decisions and gave each child so selflessly. She was loving, kind, gentle and gracious. The time frame was short, as she was due within a couple months. She wasn't asking for much financially and she was working directly with our lawyer, so all our expenses were as minimal as possible. And she was located closer to us than any of our other birth mothers. This last adoption was above and beyond what we could have hoped for with how easy it was. God knew we needed this last story to be simple, and He provided just that. *Or* had we finally learned to hold our hands open to what God set before us?

I tell the final story of adoption like this: we matched with our birth mother in January and submitted all our mountains of paperwork again. (The fourth time around we had really streamlined this process. Even our friends had saved their letters of recommendation knowing we'd most likely be crazy enough to adopt a fourth.) Then six weeks later, in February, we received a call from our lawyer that our birth mother was in labor. Due to the pandemic restrictions, this time we couldn't go to the hospital. So we continued with our day-Jon working, me pretending to work as I parented and home schooled (did I mention that we went down that rabbit hole of homeschooling three children five and under?) Then our lawyer called late afternoon saying he had been born. I hopped in the car and went up to meet him. Held his sweet self for about an hour, the maximum time allowed for visitors in the hospital, and came home and went out on a date night with

Jon, toasting the birth of our new baby boy. It was most definitely surreal to be out to dinner with Jon instead of in the hospital holding the baby. Unfortunately, the rules were such that we couldn't be there. It definitely forced us to relax and trust that our birth mother, who was there and feeding him, wouldn't change her mind. But out of all our birth mothers, I never questioned this situation. Perhaps it was because she'd placed sixth other babies without changing her mind, or perhaps it was because I'd grown in faith. We knew enough by this point to understand that if God had this baby planned for us, then it would all work out. It might sound trite, but really truly there was nothing else we could do with our hearts but trust.

After sleeping soundly all night long for the last time in awhile, I spent the day anxiously awaiting the call saying we could come pick up our new baby boy. Due to the strange pandemic rules, only one visitor was allowed in the hospital at a time, so I left Jon at home with the other three promising to return with a new baby brother for everyone. I drove the short, 30 minutes up to the hospital, and killed time grocery shopping across the street while I waited for the okay to come get him. Finally, all the final paperwork was prepped and signed, and I was called to come up and get him. I scooted across the street, up to the room, loaded his sweet self in the car seat and off I went home. Unlike the previous births, I think the entire process took about 15 minutes. I drove home, both groceries and new baby in tow, seeping in the feelings of the surreal moment. I had a new baby. I now had four children. I had ice cream that needed to get into the freezer. Logical newborn mother thoughts. When I arrived home, I handed Jon our new precious baby boy, whom he was meeting for the first time, while I unloaded groceries. I don't think a more casual adoption has ever transpired.

This is by far our most boring adoption story. But why do I bother telling it? Because it was also the most simple, straightforward, and life-giving. Adoption can be peaceful, calm, and easy. It can be all the words you wish it would be, but don't dare to hope for, because all the stories seem to be dramatic and full of angst. But it begs the question, was it the simplicity of the situation that made it so easy *or* was it that our hearts had come so far that trust led the way, letting us relax into the plans of God? If I were betting, I would definitely say the latter. It took three previous adoptions for us to finally, really, truly believe that we could trust God's plan and not try to control things ourselves. That the story He was writing would be the one that would allow us to live fully. I could have held my precious baby that first time, gone home to the date night with Jon, and spent the entire evening fretting about whether or not she'd change her mind. But I didn't. I could've talked to our lawyer that first time when I heard about the expenses, and freaked out that we'd never be able to make it work, but I didn't. I had learned that when that still small voice, the voice of God, speaks into your soul you believe it. You *listen.* You *let it sing* to your soul. And you *trust.*

This is exactly why we tell this story-often first- because of the truth it brings to others. If only everyone could learn from our hard lessons, their adoptions would also be filled with peace. If only we hadn't allowed our discontent, our worry, our desires to control our hearts in our previous stories, we would have experienced each of them so differently. If you start out relinquishing all of it to God, the peace and joy you experience in return will change you.

So we had our storybook. Girl, boy, girl, boy. We fell into a rhythm of days together as a family, learning our colors and numbers, collecting eggs from the chickens, harvesting tomatoes from way too many tomato plants, walking to my parent's and sister's houses every afternoon for tea and a visit, running wild on our dead-end street with the neighborhood children every afternoon. We were blessed, living in this amazing area, living this good life of building a family with our four adopted children and creating for them a happy and secure home, fulfilling the dreams God had placed in my heart long ago.

Then it all went up in smoke.

30

The Midlife Crisis I Didn't Want

I t was New Year's Eve, and Jon and I had wild plans to walk two doors over to spend the evening celebrating and talking of our lofty New Year's goals with our neighbors and our lively crew of nine children. That afternoon, Jon and I had been discussing where we wanted to travel, which garden to build out next, and how we needed to find more weekend getaways for just us. Our past year had been chaos and we wanted to plan this next one differently. Well, that afternoon, a thin, unassuming yet demanding fed-ex envelope had different plans in mind for us.

I remember standing in my sun-drenched living room, with the sounds of small voices in the background, opening the envelope to find a simple one-page formal letter asking us to move.

In sixty days.

To move our four young children under six. To move our floral design workshop that had 36 weddings on the books for that next year. To move away from our storybook life filled with family, friends, and a neighborhood that was irreplaceable. See, if you recall, we had been renting all this time because we had taken what would have been a down payment, four times over, and instead invested in adopting our children. Our landlords had decided they wanted to move back in and therefore we were out.

Now you might be thinking, "Just find another place." Oh how I wish it could have been that simple, but with the influx of people relocating to our area during the pandemic, the rental market had become impossible and had tripled in price. Simply put, we couldn't afford even the smallest condo in our area. We already knew this, so when I opened that letter, my heart just wrenched in two and panic started to build in my chest. Our world was turned upside down in one afternoon as it dawned on us that we would not just need to move (a seemingly monumental task), but move *out of state* to a more affordable area. We weren't just moving, we were suddenly relocating. Leaving all we knew and loved behind. This life we had so desperately fought for so we could build this family for these children, and we couldn't stay. They would no longer be walking distance from their grandparents or cousins. Their neighbors wouldn't be the lovely same-aged children we had spent the last few years loving. Tears streamed down my cheeks and my heart broke apart as I thought about their small worlds being peeled wide open. Our hand was forced and it took every ounce of our past experience and trust in God that we had built over the years, to head to our neighbor's house with an attitude of relinquishment and faith that God was going before us. That He already had gone before us, found where we would move, the community we would know, and the life we would build. We were devastated and yet we had finally learned to hold our hands open.

The further into January we crawled, with boxes piled up around us as we faithfully packed up, not even sure of where we headed, we leaned into that trust more and more. If Jon wanted to keep his job (which he most certainly did), we needed to be close to one of his company's offices. So we drew circles around each cross country office, made a list of pros and cons for each area, started looking for housing in each area, and began to pray like crazy. By mid-January we had put an offer on an inexpensive, but charming farmhouse, which we had never seen in person. Three days later we were committed. By the end of February we had moved from California....to Virginia. Our life was flipped upside down and inside out as God took us from our comfortable fairy tale world we had built and moved us to a new life across the country to a place we'd never been.

But here's what actually happened. We began to feel relief and excitement. In those first two tumultuous months, I sold off all my floral supply inventory and made plans to have my team handle weddings in my absence, and I would return only for the major ones. I began to feel a weight lifted from my shoulders. As I arranged for moving containers and purged the excess belongings, I felt my breathing come easier, my mind more at peace.

In the previous year, as the COVID restrictions had lifted and as I had begun working again, the pace of the work started to increase, making up for the lost year when the pandemic canceled all the weddings and events. Not only that, our workshop was located at our house, so I could conveniently parent and work synchronously. Our last son had been born in February, and by May, my schedule was spinning out of control. Work was at a feverish pace with more weddings than we could handle each weekend-contracts we already had on the books combined with those which had been pushed and re-booked into this year. We had just experienced the most amazingly calm and peaceful year together as a family and this was the polar opposite. We were obligated to these weddings and contracts and could do nothing about it.

I was grateful for this work, as it had helped us pay for this last adoption. However, I struggled to maintain the balance between parenting and teaching my preschoolers (the California school systems were still a mess.) That and I was still creating floral and delivering weddings with the level of perfection I had come to expect from myself and my team. My whole team would spend days in our workshop frantically churning out flower arrangements and simultaneously entertaining my children. We had not been able to find consistent childcare so all the children were with us, underfoot, "learning" how to make flower arrangements. Someone was always wearing the baby. My team shouldered so much responsibility as we struggled to make it all work. Some days we'd make close to 200 arrangements and I'd not do a single one, being torn between leading my teams, changing diapers, managing naps, feeding snacks, and entertaining small beings. Some weekends I'd have four weddings, racing between venues and our workshop, trying to keep on top of it all, being gone from seven in the morning until close to midnight. Meanwhile Jon would spend all week working and his weekend solo parenting, caring for all the children, including a five-month-old baby. It was chaos and hard and not at all the vision we had for our life. Once again we were slaves to our work. I could feel my edges fraying, my vision for our life fading. At the end of that wedding season, I was exhausted, burnt out, and terribly afraid of doing it all again the following season. Our wedding season was long, running from March until November. By Christmas, we had finally come up for air and I was looking at these four small children, longing for the peaceful pace we'd had previously experienced.

Then God stopped it all again with that simple letter in January. He redirected our path and set us back on the course to protect our family and in turn, these children's future.

So there we were in our early 40s: four children under six, a great job and a thriving floral design company, within walking distance to my parents and sister's houses, in an area where I was born and raised. A dreamworld we had fought hard to build. Years of hard work crashing down in a single afternoon. And we knew, we just *knew*, God had bigger plans for us. We held our hands open, allowed our trust to run rampant, and let Him guide us to this new place-to this new life for our family. God's plan had never been what we expected, but by now we knew it would be better.

31

This Is the End

I sat on the bed overlooking the large grassy field of our new home, tears streaming down my cheeks. I could see the children jumping wildly and gloriously, living their best lives, on the rickety trampoline left behind by the previous owners. My beautiful chickens were pecking around the field in the shade of the towering, newly vibrant, green trees that bordered our property. It looked idyllic and yet, I had just slammed the door shut against the outside world (the outside world being my four children) in frustration. Normally, this would be the moment where I would walk down the street to my parent's house with the kids in tow to let them loose to climb the trees in my parent's garden while I vented all my frustrations to my mother. But no, I was alone in this strange state, in this new town, in an old house with quirks, charms, and plenty of problems and not a soul to confide in.

But wait, my husband was just out there working in his office. My best friend with whom I had built this life and who had been my favorite *choice* long before any childcare came on the scene. But somehow in the past few years I had leaned on him less and less. I had confided in him less and less. I had turned to him less and less as I weathered parenting and midlife anxieties. The previous proximity of my parent's house had allowed me the joys of their companionship, which I loved, but I had leaned on them to the detriment of my own marriage. Now, alone in Virginia without knowing a soul, I had to return to the one person with whom I had created our story. It took our worlds being broken apart to reclaim our marriage, and in turn, build a stronger family for our children.

Everything we had dreamed our life would be was crushed, stripped away, and laid bare before God's plan. It was a devastating move for us. We loved our families, we loved our neighborhood and community, we loved our floral design company, we loved our life. And maybe if we had had just one or two children, we could have figured out how to stay and make it work. But no, we had a large family who needed space. We needed to be in a desperate place for God to move us from where we thought we were thriving, to where we needed to be. Because in all honesty, seeds of discontent with our pace and rhythm of life had started to multiply prior to our forced move. Wedges had taken root between Jon and myself, so it took everything being stripped away for us to see how we needed to build our life differently. The move away from our charmed storybook life revealed how we had become distracted from our original vision for our family.

We needed to become desperately broken so that God could open our eyes to the things that needed to change in our marriage and in our family. Years of practicing letting go of control gave both Jon and I the foresight to not fight this process, but lean into it. To see it as an opportunity no matter how challenging it was. It was definitely not easy or smooth, and many many times we looked at each other asking if we had made a mistake, but over and over again we would confirm, no, this is what God had planned for us. You see, the more you surrender your dreams and desires to God, the easier it is to leave your hands open to receive the blessings He has planned for you.

That first year in Virginia, we fought to reform our marriage and our family life. We tucked into our new home together and spent day in and day out living, breathing, and knowing each other more. Jon worked mainly from home, so the children were able to tether their days around showing him projects, found objects, creations, and silly things. And Jon and I only had each other. We repeatedly chose to turn towards each other for comfort, support, and love. We committed to a weekly date night. We ate dinner every night as a family. We did projects, repaired the house, dreamed big with each other. Again, it sounds idyllic but it was *hard* because that was all we had, each other. There weren't any other options and I am forever grateful there weren't.

What had been the original vision for our family and adopting children? To build a secure, loving, godly home where we were their safe place. A place where no matter what happened in their stories, they could and would want to return to their safe place with us for encouragement, love, and hope. In order to do that, we needed to create bonds with them that could not be easily severed. We needed to be present and consistent. We needed to be whole. We needed to have an unbreakable marriage and a family culture that was strong and unwavering. We couldn't do that at the pace our life had been, with all the intrusions coming in from all sides. God knew that. He knew we needed to be stripped bare of all distractions, forced to our knees in brokenness and desperation, so that we could focus on what was important, our family. We had to purge ourselves of past habits, rhythms, desires, and dreams so that we could see again the clear, strong bonds that God wanted for us with these children which we had promised we'd nurture into adulthood. We had been entrusted with their care, we had been called to be good stewards of their minds, their hearts and their beings. And not until we were removed from our comfortable life in California, did we see how we needed to do it differently.

So here is where our story ends, for now.

What started as deep rejection for me from multiple colleges, and placing a baby for adoption for Jon, ended with us raising four beautiful children with hearts open to God's leading. Where He would go, we would follow. He took the girl who deeply and desperately longed for a marriage and a family and took her heart on an unpredictable journey. He took me through pain, disappointment, jealousy, crushed dreams and all the other moments where I believed the threads of my life were in tatters-and then finally, I could see He was weaving the most beautiful cloth of my life. Better than I could have expected, more than I could have imagined.

What began for us as a desire to build a family, became an unexpected travel through our hearts. The life we thought we were building was shaken so off course, it was as though we had been living on the surface of the sea, not knowing the glorious depths of the ocean of our souls beneath us. God knew we wanted a fairy-tale life, but instead provided us with an epic adventure. The twists and turns, heartbreak and beauty was His plan. *This* was His purpose for our lives and for the lives of these children: a deep and profound trust in Him.

32

Feel Confident in Your Adoption

So now that you've heard our story of what led us to adoption, you most likely are wondering how this applies to you and how it will help you in your journey to build a family. Let's start with the main problem. You have a desire for a family and somehow that is not looking like you thought it would. Maybe you call it unmet desires, unfulfilled dreams, unfair life-whatever you choose to call it, it comes down to one simple thing: You are not happy with where you are and what you have. You want something else. You want more. You want a family, complete with a loving spouse and beautiful children (and that is not wrong). But it boils down to one thing: You are discontent. Maybe that's not what you call it, but that's what it is. *I'm here in this life and I want to be over there in that one.* The problem is that your discontent is robbing you-stealing your joy, usurping your sanity, wrecking any sanctuary you've created. It is killing your life.

Here's the bigger problem. You just read this story and probably experienced some level of jealousy or hatred towards our adoption stories. How do I know this? Because I have done it too. I hated the joys others experienced. Remember how I would tolerate wedding and baby showers? You and I, we're not that different. I'm betting that the joy I exuded in some of these chapters ruffled your feathers, or got your goat, or any other barnyard phrase. I'm not calling you out to shame you, I'm saying all this out loud because *I am there too.* And what it comes down to for me is the belief that I deserve joy. That in all my unmet desires (I still have them), I still long for things and struggle not to be jealous of others. Everyone *should* experience joy and contentment. I am one of those everyones, so why am I not? That's the question you ask yourself when the green seeds of envy start to plant themselves in your heart. Why am I not thriving in my life and experiencing deep joy? Because we are allowing discontentment to rob us of our story. The one designed by God that will allow us to thrive.

Here is what I urge you to do: retrace the threads of your life and see how God has prepared you and your heart. Look closely at the ways He's shaped you and molded you into being a certain person. A person that can love and care deeply, unconditionally, and wholly for a child that is not of your own flesh and blood. You will see the the pieces of your journey come together in a way you didn't know was possible. This will lead you to the answers which have been plaguing your heart, the reason you picked up this book in the first place.

Every adoption story is different. We had friends go through the process of adoption at the same time we were and their stories are so different from ours. Even while I was writing this book, I was told stories of journeys that looked nothing like mine. Was ours better? Easier? The right way to do things? No. Absolutely not. Did God prepare us specifically for our experiences? Give us the skills we needed to navigate our own challenges? Absolutely. This is why you can walk confidently forward, knowing that God has prepared you exactly for your situation. See how He has already met some of your desires and created a better pathway for your story to follow than you could have imagined.

Let me give you some examples to help make this vague idea a bit more concrete. Perhaps you have struggled with fertility for years and adoption was not your first choice. You have been longing for your *own* child, birthed from your body, filled with your DNA, with the potential to be a little mini you. Adoption is a consolation prize in your mind. You are reluctantly considering it and even, after reading all our many stories, you're not convinced.

Sit with that a minute. You are perfectly positioned to understand the deep sacrifice a birth mother will make when she places that baby in your arms. You have longed and longed for a child of your own and maybe she has too, but her circumstances are telling her that raising one would not be the wise decision. Maybe it would be unsafe or maybe she simply does not have the means to do so. So instead she puts the desires of her heart aside and allows someone else to have her dream. Since you have the same dream, you can understand the pain this must cause, the deep sacrifice she is making. You have the means and the safe environment to raise her child as she wishes she could. You are uniquely designed to understand how great a loss this would be to you; therefore, you are capable of more compassion than someone else who pursued adoption as *the* prize, desiring it from the beginning.

Does this lessen the pain of your unmet desires? No, it does not. But you can have both. You can mourn your unmet desires *and* be open to the delicate promptings of God. Do I still wish I had been married with children at a young age? Yes I do, for a variety of reasons, *but* I am also open and willing to see the journey God has me on as a better journey than what I had desired.

Perhaps you have longed to adopt but it seems like every avenue you have pursued has been a disaster. One failed adoption after another. Countless doors closed in your face. You think to yourself, here I am *longing* to adopt and yet nothing is working out for me. Trace back through the threads of your life and pay attention to what you are holding onto perhaps a bit too tightly. Were you hoping for a certain type of adoption? Looking for the story that looked like someone else's? Maybe you only wanted a girl, or only a newborn, or perhaps something quick and local, or maybe you have wanted the seemingly "perfect" child and have been put off by the situations presented to you. Or perhaps it is none of these-you've been willing to take anything that comes your way, but nothing has worked out. Rest in your desires for a minute and ask yourself, *why, why do I desire this?*

Sometimes (often) the desires of our hearts are so loud that we miss what God has already given us, *or* we miss the door that is open in front of us. We allow discontent to steal the life we are living. Jealously is a form of discontent. Maybe you were longing for an infant, but your cousin needs you to adopt their preschooler. Maybe you were hoping for a girl, but these twin boys are available. Maybe, just maybe, you long to be a parent but God has been shutting that door and has other plans for you. Plans you have not wanted to acknowledge. The moment we stop struggling to force our desires into existence, stop struggling to control our future, is the moment we start living fully and settle into a deep contentment with how God is providing and will provide for us. We all deserve joy and contentment. We have all been promised joy and contentment. We have not been promised that it will look like we expect.

This book is less about adoption and more about our hearts. About learning to relinquish control and unclench the fists that hold our desires so that we can see how God has woven our story together in a perfect plan for our lives.

This story is about a life that is not at all what we had expected. It has been so much more.